my **revision** notes

Pearson Edexcel GCSE (9–1) History

THE USA 1954–75
Conflict at home and abroad

Neil Owen

HODDER
EDUCATION
AN HACHETTE UK COMPANY

The Publishers would like to thank the following for permission to reproduce copyright material.

Acknowledgements: mark scheme based on Sample Assessment Materials (Mark Schemes): Pearson Edexcel Level 1/Level 2 GCSE (9–1) in History (1 HIO). Reproduced by kind permission of Pearson Education Ltd.

Every effort has been made to trace all copyright holders, but if any have been inadvertently overlooked, the Publishers will be pleased to make the necessary arrangements at the first opportunity.

Although every effort has been made to ensure that website addresses are correct at time of going to press, Hodder Education cannot be held responsible for the content of any website mentioned in this book. It is sometimes possible to find a relocated web page by typing in the address of the home page for a website in the URL window of your browser.

Hachette UK's policy is to use papers that are natural, renewable and recyclable products and made from wood grown in well-managed forests and other controlled sources. The logging and manufacturing processes are expected to conform to the environmental regulations of the country of origin.

Orders: please contact Hachette UK Distribution, Hely Hutchinson Centre, Milton Road, Didcot, Oxfordshire, OX11 7HH. Telephone: +44 (0)1235 827827. Email education@hachette.co.uk. Lines are open from 9 a.m. to 5 p.m., Monday to Friday. You can also order through our website: www.hoddereducation.com

ISBN: 978 1 5104 5628 0

© Neil Owen 2019

First published in 2019 by
Hodder Education
An Hachette UK Company
Carmelite House, 50 Victoria Embankment
London EC4Y 0DZ

www.hoddereducation.co.uk

Impression number 10 9 8 7 6 5 4 3

Year   2023 2022

Cover photo © Independent Picture Service/Alamy Stock Photo
Illustrations by Integra Software Services Pvt. Ltd., Pondicherry, India.
Produced and typeset by Integra Software Services Pvt. Ltd., Pondicherry, India.
Printed in India.

A catalogue record for this title is available from the British Library.

How to get the most out of this book

This book will help you revise for the modern depth study The USA, 1954–75: conflict at home and abroad.

Use the revision planner on pages 2–3 to track your progress, topic by topic. Tick each box when you have:

1 revised and understood each topic
2 completed the activities
3 checked your answers online.

The content in the book is organised into a series of double-page spreads which cover the content in the specification. The left-hand page on each spread has the key content for each topic, and the right-hand page has one or two activities to help you with exam skills or learn the knowledge you need. Answers to these activities can be found online at www.hoddereducation.co.uk/myrevisionnotesdownloads. Quick multiple-choice quizzes to test your knowledge of each topic can also be found on the website.

At the end of the book is an exam focus section (pages 40–46) which gives you guidance on how to answer each exam question type.

Tick to track your progress as you revise each element of the key content.

Key terms and **Key profiles** are highlighted in **purple** the first time they appear, with an explanation nearby in the margin. As you work through this book, highlight other key ideas and add your own notes. Make this *your* book.

Content for each topic is on the left-hand page.

Revision task: Shorter revision tasks help you remember key points of content.

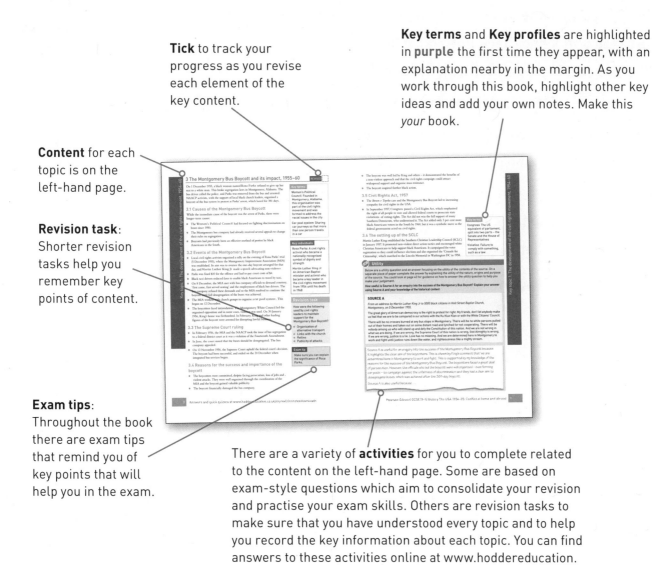

Exam tips: Throughout the book there are exam tips that remind you of key points that will help you in the exam.

There are a variety of **activities** for you to complete related to the content on the left-hand page. Some are based on exam-style questions which aim to consolidate your revision and practise your exam skills. Others are revision tasks to make sure that you have understood every topic and to help you record the key information about each topic. You can find answers to these activities online at www.hoddereducation.co.uk/myrevisionnotesdownloads.

My revision planner

REVISED

Key topic 1: The development of the civil rights movement, 1954–60

By law, black Americans were equal to white Americans and had the same rights. However, racial discrimination was a common feature of life in the 1950s. This meant that black Americans had inferior political, social and economic status, with the situation much worse in the South. Organisations campaigned to improve civil rights for black Americans.

1 The position of black Americans in the early 1950s

REVISED ☐

The contribution of black Americans to the American effort in the Second World War was considerable. Afterwards, especially as the Cold War was fought to protect 'democracy and freedom', many hoped for more quality in America. However, in reality black Americans were still treated as second-class citizens across the USA in the 1950s.

1.1 Segregation

- In many Southern states, a system of race control was in operation. This was known as the **Jim Crow Laws**.
- Southern towns were segregated into black and white areas; this included separate public places, educational institutions and transport.
- Black Americans experienced a lower economic status as they were employed mainly in agriculture as **sharecroppers** or in domestic service.
- Black Americans had little or no protections from white police officers or juries.
- In the Plessey v Ferguson case in 1896, the **Supreme Court** had judged segregation was constitutional if separate conditions for black and white Americans were equal. This promoted the idea of 'separate but equal'.

1.2 Discrimination

Many Southern white Americans believed that black Americans were racially inferior. Black Americans faced persecution from the **Ku Klux Klan** and faced widespread discrimination in housing, employment and education. As they had the worst paid jobs and often received lower wages, many black Americans lived in **ghettos**.

1.3 Voting rights in the Southern states

The right to vote was important for black Americans in order to influence politicians to pass laws to improve the circumstances they faced. Many Southern states used techniques to prevent black Americans from voting such as:

- white gangs intimidated black Americans if they tried to register to vote
- unnecessarily complex literacy tests were used to make it harder for black Americans to register to vote
- the 'Grandfather clause' (which enabled illiterate white people to vote as they could demonstrate their grandfathers had been registered) was introduced
- white employers threatened to sack black workers if they registered to vote
- a payment of a poll tax before someone registered to vote, which many black Americans couldn't afford, was enforced.

1.4 The work of civil rights organisations, including the NAACP and CORE

Many campaigned to improve civil rights and end discriminatory practices. **Pressure groups** – with membership from black and white Americans drawn from across US society – were prominent in arguing for integration. These included:

> **Key terms**
>
> **Jim Crow Laws** State and local laws, enacted from 1876–1965, that enforced racial segregation in the Southern USA
>
> **Sharecroppers** A type of farming in which families rent small plots of land from a landowner in return for a portion of their crop
>
> **Supreme Court** The highest federal court of the USA
>
> **Ku Klux Klan** Racial supremacy group, based in the South, who used violence against black Americans
>
> **Ghettos** Name given to neighbourhoods of minority ethnic communities in the USA with segregated conditions and widespread poverty
>
> **Pressure group** An organised group that does not seek election, but which tries to influence and change government policy
>
> **Non-violent direct action** Rejecting violence in favour of peaceful tactics as a means of gaining political objectives

- The National Association for the Advancement of Colored People (NAACP), which was established in 1909 with the aim of using all legal means to achieve equality and end the 'separate but equal' ruling.
- The Congress of Racial Equality (CORE), which was established in 1942 and used **non-violent direct action** to demand the end of segregation.

Revision task

Summarise the role played by the following groups in the civil rights movement:

- NAACP
- CORE

Exam tip

Make sure you thoroughly revise the issue of voting rights and can describe the obstacles black Americans faced in trying to register to vote.

 You're the examiner

1   Below are an exam-style question, a mark scheme and a paragraph written in answer to the question. Read the paragraph and the mark scheme and decide what mark you would give the answer.

Give **two** things you can infer from Source A about segregation in the Southern states. (4 marks)

SOURCE A

From Martin Luther King's book, Stride Toward Freedom: The Montgomery Story, *in which he describes how racial segregation was organised on buses in Alabama.*

Frequently Negroes paid their fare at the front door, and then were forced to get off and reboard at the rear. An even more humiliating practice was the custom of forcing Negroes to stand over empty seats reserved for 'whites only'. Even if the bus had no white passengers, and Negroes were packed throughout, they were prohibited from sitting in the front four seats (which held ten persons). But the practice went further. If white persons were already occupying all of their reserved seats and additional white people boarded the bus. Negroes sitting in the unreserved section immediately behind the whites were asked to stand so that the whites could be seated. If the Negroes refused to stand and move back, they were arrested.

Mark scheme	
2 marks	1 mark for each valid inference up to a maximum of two inferences
2 marks	The second mark for each inference is for supporting detail selected from the source

STUDENT ANSWER

The source suggests that many black Americans were physically segregated on buses. The source also suggests that the police supported segregation.

Mark ☐   Reason _____

_____

2   Now write an answer which could gain four marks.

2 Progress in education

Segregation and discrimination in education meant black Americans had limited opportunities. Black Americans were not allowed to attend white schools, which were often far superior to black schools.

2.1 The key features of the *Brown v Topeka* case (1954)

- Church Minister Oliver Brown challenged segregated schools in Topeka, Kansas. Brown wanted his daughter, Linda, to attend a local school, rather than the all-black school located some distance away.
- The NAACP – led by lawyer **Thurgood Marshall** – supported Brown in his appeal to the Supreme Court.
- Marshall argued that segregation was against the **Fourteenth Amendment**, as segregation made black children feel unequal.
- The process took 18 months and the Supreme Court ruled on 17 May 1954 to oppose segregated education.

2.2 The immediate and long-term significance of the case

- The ruling overturned the 1896 *Plessy v Ferguson* decision which allowed public facilities to be segregated.
- The case was a victory for the NAACP and the tactics it had pursued. It had long campaigned against segregated education.
- Acceptance of the ruling varied. The Supreme Court didn't give a deadline by which desegregation had to be achieved. It stated later that integration had to be accomplished 'with all deliberate speed', believing that schools needed time to adjust.
- It fuelled an extreme white backlash and led to a rise in popularity of the Ku Klux Klan.
- White Citizens' Councils were formed to defend segregation and there was significant resistance to it in many Southern states. Many Southern politicians signed the Southern Manifesto which committed them to fight against the Brown decision.
- **President Dwight Eisenhower** did little to encourage integration.

2.3 The events at Little Rock High School, 1957

- After the *Brown v Topeka* decision, desegregation of education began in Little Rock, the state capital of Arkansas.
- Nine black students tried to enrol at the Little Rock High School on 3 September 1957, the start of the new term. State governor **Orval Faubus** opposed this and ordered Arkansas State National Guardsmen to prevent the students from entering the school.
- The nine students, led by Elizabeth Eckford, arrived together on 4 September, where they were met by a mob of white people who tried to stop them entering the school. The watching press recorded these events, which were broadcast across the world.
- President Eisenhower was forced to act, not least to protect the USA's image abroad. He took control of the **National Guard** and sent in troops to protect the black students and to force the state to obey the law.
- The troops remained until the end of the term to ensure the safety of the 'Little Rock Nine'. However, the threats continued and when the school year ended Faubus closed every Little Rock school for the next school year, to prevent integration. Schools reopened in 1959, but only after a Supreme Court ruling.

Key terms

Fourteenth Amendment Passed in 1868, the Fourteenth Amendment of the US Constitution declares citizenship to all people that are either born in or nationalised in the USA

National Guard A reserve military force of US soldiers and airmen

Key individuals

Thurgood Marshall A civil rights advocate and later US Supreme Court justice

President Dwight Eisenhower US President from 1953 to 1961

Orval Faubus Governor of Arkansas from 1955 to 1967 and an opponent of integration

2.4 The significance of the events at Little Rock High School, 1957

- The events at Little Rock showed that the Supreme Court rulings were not popularly received. Following Little Rock, Faubus was re-elected a further four times. This made many within the civil rights movement realise that they had to do more than simply rely on court decisions if they were to secure advancements for black Americans.
- Authorities were not keen to enforce *Brown v Topeka*. It was not until 1972 that Little Rock's schools were fully integrated. By 1964, only 3 per cent of black children attended desegregated schools.
- Little Rock drew national attention and helped influence moderate white opinion, as many US citizens saw the extent of the racial hatred that existed in Southern states.
- The involvement of the President and the federal government showed that the issue of civil rights was now at the heart of US politics.

Revision task

Compare the attitudes and actions of President Eisenhower on the issue of civil rights, compared to those of Presidents Kennedy, Johnson and Nixon.

Exam tip

Make sure you know the precise details about the events at Little Rock High School in 1957.

 ## RAG: Rate the timeline

Below are an exam-style question and a timeline. Read the question, study the timeline and, using three coloured pens, put a **red**, **amber** or **green** star next to the events to show:

Red: events and policies that have **no** relevance to the question

Amber: events and policies that have **some** relevance to the question

Green: events and policies that have **direct** relevance to the question.

Explain why the Little Rock crisis helped progress the civil rights movement.

You may use the following in your answer:
- The role of the President
- International outrage

You **must** also use information of your own.

4 Sept
Little Rock Nine try to enter the high school building and are turned away by National Guard, called in by Governor Orval Faubus

9 Sept
Judge Ronald Davies of the US District Court begins injunction proceedings against the governor and two National Guardsmen for interfering with integration

27 May
The oldest of the Little Rock Nine, Ernest Green, is the first black student to graduate from the Central High School

June 1959
A federal court rules Faubus's actions unconstitutional, forcing him to reopen the high schools

1954
US Supreme Court calls for desegregation of public schools in *Brown v Topeka*

3 Sept
NAACP try to enrol nine black students in Little Rock Central High School

8 May
Eisenhower orders National Guard to be removed from Central High School

1954	1955	1956	1957	1958	1959

1955
Little Rock school board agrees to comply with ruling

14 Sept
Faubus meets with President Eisenhower

25 Sept
Little Rock Nine successfully enter the Central High School

Sept
Faubus signs a recently passed law allowing him to close all Little Rock public high schools, forcing all students to study elsewhere

24 Sept
Eisenhower sends the US Army to Little Rock, and federalised the National Guard, removing them from Faubus's control

27 Nov
US Army leaves Little Rock

3 The Montgomery Bus Boycott and its impact, 1955–60

REVISED

On 1 December 1955, a black woman named **Rosa Parks** refused to give up her seat to a white man. This broke segregation laws in Montgomery, Alabama. The bus driver called the police, and Parks was removed from the bus and arrested. NAACP activists, with the support of local black church leaders, organised a boycott of the bus system in protest at Parks' arrest, which lasted for 381 days.

3.1 Causes of the Montgomery Bus Boycott

While the immediate cause of the boycott was the arrest of Parks, there were longer-term causes:

- The **Women's Political Council** had focused on fighting discrimination on buses since 1950.
- The Montgomery bus company had already received several appeals to change their rules on segregation.
- Boycotts had previously been an effective method of protest by black Americans in the South.

3.2 Events of the Montgomery Bus Boycott

- Local civil rights activists organised a rally on the evening of Rosa Parks' trial (5 December 1955), where the Montgomery Improvement Association (MIA) was established. Its aim was to oversee the one-day boycott arranged for that day, and **Martin Luther King Jr** made a speech advocating non-violence.
- Parks was fined $10 for the offence and had to pay court costs of $4.
- Black taxi drivers reduced fares to enable black Americans to travel by taxi.
- On 8 December, the MIA met with bus company officials to demand courtesy, 'first come, first served seating' and the employment of black bus drivers. The bus company refused these demands and so the MIA resolved to continue the boycott until full desegregation of the buses was achieved.
- The MIA worked with church groups to organise a **car pool system**. This began on 12 December.
- The boycotters faced intimidation. The Montgomery White Council led the organised opposition and in some cases, violence was used. On 30 January 1956, King's home was firebombed. In February, King and other leading figures of the boycott were arrested for disrupting lawful business.

3.3 The Supreme Court ruling

- In February 1956, the MIA and the NAACP took the issue of bus segregation to a federal district court as it was a violation of the Fourteenth Amendment.
- In June, the court stated that the buses should be desegregated. The bus company appealed.
- On 13 November 1956, the Supreme Court upheld the federal court's decision. The boycott had been successful, and ended on the 20 December when integrated bus services began.

3.4 Reasons for the success and importance of the boycott

- The boycotters were committed, despite facing persecution, loss of jobs and violent attacks. They were well organised through the coordination of the MIA and the boycott gained valuable publicity.
- The boycott financially damaged the bus company.

Key terms

Women's Political Council Founded in Montgomery, Alabama, this organisation was part of the civil rights movement and was formed to address the racial issues in the city

Car pool system Sharing car journeys so that more than one person travels in a car

Key individuals

Rosa Parks A civil rights activist who became a nationally-recognised symbol of dignity and strength

Martin Luther King Jr An American Baptist minister and activist who became a key leader in the civil rights movement from 1954 until his death in 1968

Revision task

How were the following used by civil rights leaders to maintain support for the Montgomery Bus Boycott?

- Organisation of alternative transport
- Links with the church
- Rallies
- Publicity of attacks

Exam tip

Make sure you can explain the significance of Rosa Parks.

- The boycott was well led by King and others – it demonstrated the benefits of a non-violent approach and that the civil rights campaign could attract widespread support and organise mass resistance.
- The boycott inspired further black action.

3.5 Civil Rights Act, 1957

- The *Brown v Topeka* case and the Montgomery Bus Boycott led to increasing sympathy for civil rights in the USA.
- In September 1957, **Congress** passed a Civil Rights Act, which emphasised the right of all people to vote and allowed federal courts to prosecute state **violations** of voting rights. The Act did not win the full support of many Southern Democrats, who undermined it. The Act added only 3 per cent more black Americans voters in the South by 1960, but it was a symbolic move as the federal government acted on civil rights.

3.6 The setting up of the SCLC

Martin Luther King established the Southern Christian Leadership Council (SCLC) in January 1957. It promoted non-violent direct action tactics and encouraged white Christian Americans to help support black Americans. It campaigned for voter registration so they could influence elections and also organised the 'Crusade for Citizenship', which marched to the Lincoln Memorial in Washington DC in 1958.

> **Key terms**
>
> **Congress** The US equivalent of parliament, split into two parts – the Senate and the House of Representatives
>
> **Violation** Failure to comply with something, such as a law

 Utility

Below are a utility question and an answer focusing on the utility of the contents of the source. On a separate piece of paper complete the answer by explaining the utility of the nature, origins and purpose of the source. You could look at page 43 for guidance on how to answer the utility question to help you make your judgement.

How useful is Source A for an enquiry into the success of the Montgomery Bus Boycott? Explain your answer using Source A and your knowledge of the historical context.

SOURCE A

From an address by Martin Luther King Jr to 5000 black citizens in Holt Street Baptist Church, Montgomery, on 5 December 1955.

The great glory of American democracy is the right to protest for right. My friends, don't let anybody make us feel that we are to be compared in our actions with the Ku Klux Klan or with the White Citizens' Council.

There will be no crosses burned at any bus stops in Montgomery. There will be no white persons pulled out of their homes and taken out on some distant road and lynched for not cooperating. There will be nobody among us who will stand up and defy the Constitution of this nation. And we are not wrong in what we are doing. If we are wrong, the Supreme Court of this nation is wrong, God Almighty is wrong. If we are wrong, justice is a lie. Love has no meaning. And we are determined here in Montgomery to work and fight until justice runs down like water, and righteousness like a mighty stream.

Source A is useful for an enquiry into the success of the Montgomery Bus Boycott because it highlights the clear aim of the boycotters. This is shown by King's comment that 'we are determined here in Montgomery to work and fight'. This is supported by my knowledge of the reasons for the success of the Montgomery Bus Boycott. The boycotters faced a great deal of persecution. However, the officials who led the boycott were well organised – even forming car pools – to campaign against the unfairness of discrimination and they had a clear aim to desegregate buses, which was achieved after the 381-day boycott.

Source A is also useful because …

4 Opposition to the civil rights movement

4.1 The Ku Klux Klan and violence

The Ku Klux Klan (KKK) was active in the Southern states and violently opposed the civil rights movement. Most of its members were White Anglo-Saxon Protestants (WASPs) and they saw themselves as superior to other races. Members of the KKK carried out **lynching** of black Americans. The activities of the KKK were rarely punished as some of its members also worked in law enforcement professions.

4.2 The murder of Emmett Till

- On 28 August 1955, the body of Emmett Till, a 14-year-old black American boy from Chicago was found in Money, Mississippi.
- He had been visiting relatives and had wolf-whistled Carolyn Bryant, a white woman in a grocery store, then said 'bye, baby'.
- The next night, Bryant's husband and his half-brother went to Till's uncle's house, abducted Emmett, beat and mutilated him before shooting him and throwing him in the river.
- Emmett's mother, Mamie Bradley, decided to return the body to Chicago and leave the coffin open so people could see how badly beaten he was – she wanted to expose the rest of America to the realities of life in Mississippi.
- The court case that followed was the first time that white men were charged with murdering a black man in Mississippi.
- The all-white **jury** delivered a 'not guilty' verdict – after one hour. The case attracted huge publicity and encouraged many to become civil rights activists.

4.3 Opposition to desegregation in the South

- Campaigns to desegregate the South faced opposition to block any changes.
- Some state governments in the South used their powers to maintain segregation and make it difficult to enforce the *Brown v Topeka* decision.

4.4 The setting up of White Citizens' Councils

White Citizens' Councils were groups of white people who worked to defend segregation. They had been set up to fight the *Brown v Topeka* decision, and by the mid-1950s enjoyed a membership of around 250,000. The Councils challenged desegregation plans in the law courts, as well as using violence and political and economic pressure to achieve their aims.

4.5 Congress and the 'Dixiecrats'

Attempts through the federal government to introduce and pass civil rights legislation were constantly blocked by Southern members in Congress. Desegregation was also made more difficult by the prominence of the 'Dixiecrats'. The Dixiecrats:

- were white southern **Democrats** who were opposed to desegregation
- had strong views on protecting the rights of states to retain their own laws (which in the South often guaranteed white supremacy)
- held significant influence in Congress, as the President needed their support to pass legislation.

Key terms

Lynching Punishing a person without legal process or authority, often with brutality

Jury A body of people sworn to give a verdict in a legal case on the basis of evidence submitted to them in court

Democrats One of the two major contemporary political parties in the USA, along with the Republican Party

Revision task

Give two reasons why people became members of the Ku Klux Klan.

Exam tip

Make sure you are able to demonstrate a thorough understanding of the events and impact of Emmett Till's murder.

Inference

An inference is a message that you can get from a source by reading between the lines. Below are an exam-style inference question, the source and a series of statements. Decide which of the statements:

- make(s) inferences from the source (I)
- describes what it can see in the source (D)
- cannot be justified from the source (X).

Give two things you can infer from Source A about the impact of the lynching of Emmett Till.

SOURCE A

From The Greatest: My Own Story *by Muhammad Ali, published in 2015.*

Emmett Till and I were about the same age. A week after he was murdered ... I stood on the corner with a gang of boys, looking at pictures of him in the black newspapers and magazines. In one, he was laughing and happy. In the other, his head was swollen and bashed in, his eyes bulging out of their sockets and his mouth twisted and broken. His mother had done a bold thing. She refused to let him be buried until hundreds of thousands marched past his open casket in Chicago and looked down at his mutilated body. [I] felt a deep kinship to him when I learned he was born the same year and day I was. My father talked about it at night and dramatized the crime. I couldn't get Emmett out of my mind ...

Statement	I	D	X
The Emmett Till case was a news story in the US press			
Emmett Till's body was badly beaten			
Emmett Till's family lived in Chicago			
Many people felt sympathetic towards Emmett Till's family			
Many people were appalled at Emmett Till's brutal murder			
Many black Americans became involved in the civil rights movement as a result of Emmett Till's murder			
Many people in Chicago visited Emmett Till's body			

Key topic 1: The development of the civil rights movement, 1954–60

Key topic 2: Protest, progress and radicalism, 1960–75

During the period 1960 to 1975, support for the civil rights movement grew. Non-violent direct action protests helped ignite a white reaction which earned the campaigners public sympathy and support. However, the tactics of non-violent direct action were soon criticised by some black Americans who wanted the campaign for civil rights to accelerate at a faster and broader pace.

1 Progress, 1960–62

REVISED

1.1 The significance of Greensboro and the sit-in movement

- In Greensboro, North Carolina, on 1 February 1960, four black college students from an all-black college asked to be served at an all-white lunch counter at Woolworth. They were refused service because they were black and were asked to leave. The students refused to leave and sat at the lunch counter until closing time.

- The next day, more students took part in a sit-in at the Woolworth's food counter. By the fifth day, there were 300. During these sit-ins, the students faced violence and intimidation.

- The sit-ins attracted publicity (many Americans were horrified by the violent response to them) and soon spread to other Greensboro segregated lunch counters.

- The Woolworth store at Greensboro eventually agreed to desegregate its food counter in July 1960, having lost significant business.

- The Student Non-violent Co-ordinating Committee (SNCC) was formed in 1960 with the aim of using non-violent protest to campaign for civil rights, and to continue to organise support to fight against segregated lunch counters.

1.2 The Freedom Riders

During the spring of 1961, student activists from the Congress of Racial Equality (CORE) launched **Freedom Riders** to challenge segregation that persisted despite Supreme Court rulings on interstate buses and bus terminals. Thirteen volunteers, including **James Farmer**, left Washington on 4 May 1961, for Georgia, Alabama and Mississippi.

1.3 The Anniston bomb

When the Freedom Riders got to Alabama, one of the buses was firebombed outside Anniston, on Sunday 14 May 1961. The Riders faced violence and intimidation. When the Freedom Riders reached Birmingham, they were again attacked by an angry mob. The local police chief, **Eugene 'Bull' Connor**, ordered the police not to stop the mob.

1.4 Ku Klux Klan violence

The Freedom Riders continued throughout the summer, as did the attacks on them by the KKK. The federal government did not stop the arrests. The attacks provoked wide press coverage, which helped ensure the Freedom Rides increased awareness of the civil rights campaign. In 1983, documents revealed that at the time of the attacks the FBI was aware of the KKK's plans and had decided not to arrest any KKK members, no matter how severely they attacked the Freedom Riders.

Key term

Freedom Riders Civil rights activists who rode interstate buses into the Southern states in 1961 to challenge segregated bus terminals

---

Key individuals

James Farmer Civil rights leader, National Director of CORE and organiser of the 1961 Freedom Rides

Eugene 'Bull' Connor Southern Democrat politician who served as the public safety commissioner in Birmingham, Alabama

James Meredith Became the first black American student at the University of Mississippi

---

Revision task

Summarise the similarities and differences in the reaction of white people to the Greensboro sit-in, the Freedom Riders and the James Meredith case.

1.5 The James Meredith case, 1962

- In June 1962, **James Meredith** re-applied to the University of Mississippi, which had rejected him on racial grounds in May 1961.

- The Supreme Court ordered the university to accept him, a decision which university officials refused to accept. Meredith was physically prevented from registering at the university.

- President Kennedy ordered 320 federal marshals to escort Meredith to the campus. This led to a riot in which two people were killed and many marshals and demonstrators were injured.

- Kennedy appealed for calm, while sending troops to restore order.

- Meredith registered on 1 October 1962. Troops remained on the campus until Meredith graduated three years later.

Exam tip

Remember to focus on the highly organised nature of the civil rights movement in arranging the non-violent direct action protests.

 Inference

An inference is a message that you can get from a source by reading between the lines. Below are an exam-style inference question, the source and a series of statements. Decide which of the statements:

- make(s) inferences from the source (I)
- paraphrase(s) the source (P)
- summarise(s) the source (S)
- cannot be justified from the source (X).

Give two things you can infer from Source A about the Freedom Rides.

SOURCE A

James Peck, a member of the Freedom Rides, writing about his experiences in Alabama on 14 May 1961, in his book, Freedom Ride, *first published in 1962.*

When the Greyhound bus pulled into Anniston, it was immediately surrounded by an angry mob armed with iron bars. They set about the vehicle, denting the sides, breaking windows, and slashing tires. Finally, the police arrived and the bus managed to depart. But the mob pursued in cars. Within minutes, the pursuing mob was hitting the bus with iron bars. The rear window was broken and a bomb was hurled inside. All the passengers managed to escape before the bus burst into flames and was totally destroyed. Policemen, who had been standing by, belatedly came on the scene. A couple of them fired into the air. The mob dispersed and the injured were taken to a local hospital.

Statement	I	P	S	X
The police were reluctant to protect the Freedom Riders from the mob				
The Freedom Riders faced violent opposition				
Opposition to the Freedom Riders was widespread in the South				
The Freedom Riders' bus was attacked				
The Freedom Riders wanted to create a crisis to force the government to respond				
Racists in Alabama attacked the bus passengers with clubs and chains				
The Freedom Rides were highly publicised				

2 Peaceful protests and their impact, 1963–65 (Part 1)

REVISED

By 1963, civil rights campaigners felt that a new strategy was needed to attract publicity and force change.

2.1 King and events in Birmingham, Alabama

- The SCLC sought to end segregation in Birmingham, Alabama with a new campaign – Project C (confrontation) – to achieve maximum publicity across the USA.
- Birmingham was still completely segregated – Martin Luther King described Birmingham as 'the most segregated city in the United States' – and felt Police Chief Eugene 'Bull' Connor could be provoked to use violence against peaceful protesters.
- The demonstrations began on 3 April 1963. The Birmingham campaign included sit-ins, meetings, protest marches and boycotts.
- The police response was as expected. King was among the hundreds of protesters who were arrested in the first few weeks. Up to 900 children were arrested for joining the marches. When the jails were full, Connor ordered the police to set dogs on the protesters and used water hoses to disperse the demonstrators. These images were widely broadcasted, gaining the publicity King had wanted.
- President Kennedy sent his Assistant **Attorney General** to resolve the tensions and restore order as the events in Birmingham had 'damaged America'.
- Talks between King and the Birmingham city leaders were successful, and an agreement was reached on 9 May 1963, which stated that desegregation would occur in Birmingham within 90 days.

2.2 King and the peace march on Washington

After the success of Birmingham, the civil rights leaders wanted to maintain pressure for a Civil Rights Bill. They planned to commemorate the centenary of the freeing of enslaved black Americans in 1863 with a huge protest march to campaign for jobs and freedom. Washington, as the political capital of the USA, was chosen as the destination for the march. This was organised by the NAACP, CORE, SNCC and SCLC. Over 250,000 demonstrators, including many white Americans, from all across the USA, took part in a peaceful march which was broadcast live on television. King was the final speaker of the day and made his famous 'I have a dream' speech. The march was a success and put further pressure on President Kennedy to act on civil rights.

2.3 Freedom Summer

- In 1964, SNCC and CORE worked together to organise the Freedom Summer in Mississippi. They also created the Mississippi Freedom Party (MFDP) to help boost voter registration and to protest against segregation.
- The MFDP established 30 **Freedom Schools** to help address racial inequalities. The schools were run by volunteers, including 1000 who were white college students.
- The schools and volunteers became the subject of white racist attacks. The KKK burned crosses, churches and homes to demonstrate their opposition, in addition to physically attacking the volunteers.

Key terms

Attorney General Head of the US Department of Justice and chief lawyer of the US government

Freedom Schools Temporary, alternative free schools for black Americans which aimed to encourage them to become more politically active

Revision task

Summarise the methods of the various methods used by the peaceful protestors to attract publicity and force change.

2.4 The Mississippi murders

- On 21 June 1964 three Freedom Summer activists (Michael Schwerner, Andrew Goodman and James Chaney) were arrested. Upon their release later that day, they were murdered by the Ku Klux Klan, following a tip-off by a police officer who was a KKK member. Their bodies were not located until 4 August.
- The murders became a scandal which caused public outrage.

Exam tip

You must be able to explain the significance of the March on Washington in attracting wider publicity for the civil rights campaign.

 Inference

Below are an exam-style question and part of an answer.

Give two things you can infer from Source A (below) about the events of Birmingham, 1963.

> Civil rights campaigners in Birmingham faced violent attacks to their peaceful protests. The details from the source which support this are the references to 'vicious mobs lynch'.

Now make a second inference and use details from the source to support it.

 Utility

Use the questions and statements in the white boxes around Source A to make notes in answer to the following question:

How useful is Source A for an enquiry into the attitudes of the civil rights leaders in 1963? Explain your answer, using Source A and your knowledge of the historical context.

What is useful about the contents of the source?

Contextual knowledge to support your answer

What is useful about the nature, origins or purpose of the source?

SOURCE A

From Martin Luther King's 'Letter from Birmingham Jail' (1963).

But when you have seen vicious mobs lynch your mothers and fathers at will and drown your brothers and sisters at whim; when you see the vast majority of your twenty million Negro brothers smothering in an airtight cage of poverty in the midst of an affluent society; when you are harried by day and haunted by night by the fact that you are a Negro ... when you are forever fighting a degenerating sense of nobodiness, then you will understand why we find it difficult to wait.

2 Peaceful protests and their impact, 1963–65 (Part 2)

2.5 The role of Presidents Kennedy and Johnson

- Both presidents appointed black Americans to high-level government and judiciary jobs, used **executive orders** to send in federal troops and backed the Civil Rights Bill.

- President Kennedy's achievements were limited as he feared losing the support of the Dixiecrats.

- President Johnson, a Southerner from Texas, promoted the vision of the **'Great Society'**, and believed racial reform would help the economic, political and spiritual reintegration of the South within America.

2.6 Civil Rights Act, 1964

The 1964 Civil Rights Act was signed on 2 July, and reflected the changing public mood on civil rights. The Act banned segregation in public places. It also banned job discrimination, which was to be enforced by a newly established Equal Opportunities Commission. However, the Act failed to address the issue of voting registration or the poverty Black Americans suffered.

2.7 Selma

- Unhappy with the limitations to the Civil Rights Act, King and other civil rights leaders organised another non-violent campaign.

- Selma, Alabama, was chosen because around 50 per cent of its population were black Americans, but fewer than 1 per cent of the black population were registered to vote. King said that Selma 'has become a symbol of bitter-end resistance to the civil rights movement in the Deep South.'

- Selma's police chief, Jim Clark, was a hardliner. He would deal brutally with any civil rights opposition and this would help attract national publicity.

- The campaign began in January 1965. King and his followers were subjected to beatings and arrests.

- On Sunday 7 March, about 600 protesters marched from Selma to Montgomery (Alabama's capital) to present a petition asking for voting rights to Governor Wallace.

- In an event known as 'Bloody Sunday', as the marchers crossed the Pettus Bridge out of the city, they were attacked with tear gas and clubs and forced to return to Selma.

- President Johnson used an executive order to **federalise** the state national guard, who escorted the march from Selma to Montgomery on 21–24 March. King led more than 25,000 people – the biggest march ever seen in the South.

2.8 Voting Rights Act, 1965

- The Selma campaign and the national (and international) criticism of the events of Bloody Sunday that followed, put pressure on President Johnson to act.

- On 6 August 1965, President Johnson signed the Voting Rights Act.

- The Act introduced one voting registration requirement and established federal officials to monitor voter registration.

- It outlawed literacy tests and poll taxes as a way of assessing whether a person was fit to vote.

- By the end of 1966, only four of the thirteen Southern states had fewer than 50 per cent of black Americans registered to vote.

Key terms

Executive order A directive issued by the president of the USA that manages operations of the federal government and has the force of law

'Great Society' A series of programmes, with a focus on ending poverty and racial injustice, which were set up on the initiative of President Johnson

Federalise To put under the direct control and authority of a federal government

Revision task

Draw a timeline of civil rights protests from 1960 to 1965.

Exam tip

You must be able to explain why the Voting Rights Act of 1965 was so important.

Eliminate irrelevance

Below is an exam-style question:

Explain why there was progress in the civil rights movement, 1963–1965.

Below is part of an answer to the question above. Some parts of the answer are not relevant to the question. Identify these and draw a line through the information that is irrelevant, justifying your deletions in the margin.

> You may use the following in your answer:
> ■ Role of the presidents
> ■ Selma March
>
> **You must also use information of your own.**

One reason why there was progress in the civil rights movement was because of the role of the presidency. Both President Kennedy and, after his assassination on 22 November 1963 in Dallas, Texas, his successor, President Johnson, were important figures in passing new civil rights legislation. Despite voting against President Eisenhower's Civil Rights Bill in 1957, during the presidential campaign and after he was nominated for the Democrats, Kennedy made it clear in his speeches that he was a supporter of civil rights. Both Presidents were sensitive to the fact that racial discrimination stained America as it led the West's stance against the Soviet Union during the Cold War. Both Kennedy and Johnson did more than any president before them to have more black Americans appointed to federal government posts.

Another reason why there was progress in the civil rights movement was because of the impact of the Selma march. The Selma to Montgomery march was part of a series of civil rights protests that occurred in 1965 in Alabama. The troopers fired tear gas and protesters were beaten, set upon by dogs and charged with horses. Some 2000 people set out from Selma on 21 March, protected by US Army troops and Alabama National Guard forces that President Johnson had ordered under federal control. After walking some 12 hours a day and sleeping in fields along the way, they reached Montgomery on 25 March. The historic march, and Martin Luther King Jr's participation in it, raised national and international awareness through the mass media of the difficulties faced by black American voters, and the need for a national Voting Rights Act.

Choosing a third cause

To answer the question in the eliminate irrelevance activity above, you need to explain three causes. It is sensible to make use of the two given points. However, you will need to add one of your own. In the spaces below write down your choice and the reasons behind it.

Reason:

_____

_____

Why I have chosen this reason:

_____

_____

Details to support this reason:

_____

_____

_____

3 Malcolm X and Black Power, 1963–70

Following the civil rights organisations' fight for desegregation and voting rights in the South, another strand of the civil rights movement was developing in the North which sought black **separatism**.

3.1 Malcolm X, his beliefs, methods and involvement with Black Muslims

- Born Malcom Little in 1925 in Omaha, Nebraska.
- His father was murdered in 1931 by white supremacists and his early life was dominated by crime.
- When in prison, he converted to the Muslim faith, changed his name to Malcom X and joined the **Nation of Islam** (NOI).
- Malcom X became the most famous member of the NOI.

3.2 Malcolm X's later change of attitude and assassination

- In 1964, Malcolm X left the NOI. He went on a pilgrimage to Mecca. He established the Muslim Mosque Inc. and the Organization of Afro-American Unity.
- He rejected his earlier beliefs about separatism, was more willing to work with other civil rights campaigners and attacked the ideas of the NOI.
- Malcom X was assassinated by gunmen from the NOI on 21 February 1965.

3.3 Reasons for the emergence of Black Power

The emergence of Black Power was a result of a number of factors. Some felt increasingly frustrated over the slow progress of non-violent direct action, which was not leading to rapid enough change. There was also growing anger at employment and education discrimination. Black Power was also attractive for many as it emphasised the need for black Americans to be proud of their own heritage.

3.4 The significance of Stokely Carmichael

Stokely Carmichael had been active in the civil rights movement and promoted non-violent direct action. Following his election as national chairman of SNCC in May 1966, Carmichael helped to radicalise the organisation. He was a militant leader and endorsed Black Power.

3.5 The 1968 Mexico Olympics

- **Tommie Smith** and **John Carlos** staged a silent protest against racial discrimination by bowing their heads and raising a black-gloved hand as the US national anthem played during their victory ceremony.
- It was a huge shock and as they left the podium at the end of the ceremony they were booed by many in the crowd.
- It attracted worldwide attention to the Black Panther cause.

3.6 The methods and achievements of the Black Panther movement

- The Black Panther Party was established in Oakland, California, in October 1966 by Huey Newton and Bobby Searle.
- In addition to adopting a **ten-point programme** in October 1966, the Black Panthers wore a **paramilitary** uniform, with black beret, trousers and leather jacket.

Key terms

Separatism Keeping races apart

Nation of Islam Also known as Black Muslims, they believed in separatism from white society, pride in their heritage and armed self-defence. Members rejected their slave surnames and called themselves 'X'

Ten-point programme A list of the demands of the Black Panthers

Paramilitary Often an illegal group, similar in formation to an army

Chapters Separate branches of the Black Panther movement

Key individuals

Tommie Smith Gold medal winner in the 1968 Olympic Games, whose actions during the medal ceremony brought world attention to the Black Power movement

John Carlos Bronze medal winner in the 1968 Olympic Games, who saluted during the medal ceremony to show black unity

Revision task

Why were the following important for the Black Panthers?

- Black Power salute in the 1968 Olympics
- Malcom X
- Ten-point programme
- Stokely Carmichael

Answers and quick quizzes at www.hoddereducation.co.uk/myrevisionnotesdownloads

- Their **chapters** were based mostly in urban areas, on the West coast and in major northern cities.
- The Black Panthers exposed police brutality against black Americans by following police cars in the ghettos.
- They worked to support people living in ghettos by setting up clinics to advise on health, welfare and legal rights, as well as setting up a Free Breakfast programme for poorer people.
- However, the Black Panthers' military tactics and violent confrontations with police also led to diminished support over time.

> **Exam tip**
>
> Remember that the Black Panthers were largely based in the cities and their work focused on improving living conditions in the ghetto communities.

Strengths and weaknesses

1 Using the information on pages 18–19, copy and complete both sides of the scales to show the strengths and weaknesses of the Black Power movement.

2 Do you think the strengths outweigh the weaknesses? Give reasons for your answer.

Organising knowledge

Use the information on pages 18–19 to complete the table below to summarise the key developments in the civil rights movement which led to a change to more extreme methods in the years 1963 to 1970.

Factor	Summary
Nation of Islam	
Role of Malcom X	
Emergence of Black Power	
Stokely Carmichael	
The Black Panthers	

4 The civil rights movement, 1965–75

4.1 The riots of 1965–67

In the mid-1960s, growing anger erupted in the ghettos across America. On 11 August 1965, the Watts riot occurred in the predominantly black neighbourhood of Los Angeles. The five days of violence left 34 dead, 1032 injured, nearly 4000 arrested and $40 million worth of property destroyed. Between 1965 and 1967, summer riots – mainly in the major northern cities – killed more than 130 people and caused damage totalling more than $700 million.

4.2 Kerner Report, 1968

- In July 1967, President Johnson set up a **National Advisory Commission on Civil Disorders**, chaired by **Otto Kerner**, to investigate the factors which caused the riots.

- The Kerner Report, published in February 1968, blamed white racism for sparking the riots.

- It declared that 'Our nation is moving toward two societies, one black, one white – separate and unequal', and called for expanded aid to African American communities in order to prevent further racial violence, segregation and discrimination.

4.3 King's campaign in the North

- Following a visit to the Los Angeles Watts ghetto after the 1965 riot, King and the SCLC were increasingly aware of the need for civil rights to focus on securing economic justice for black Americans.

- In Chicago – a northern city with a large black population – King established the Chicago Freedom Movement which aimed to remove segregation.

- He used the same non-violent direct action tactics used in the South.

- These tactics were not effective – he was attacked as a **communist**, he did not receive the support of Mayor **Richard Daley** and his marches provoked violent responses which led to unfavourable publicity.

- King's interest in the North lessened as he became more involved in the anti-Vietnam War movement.

4.4 The assassination of Martin Luther King and its impact

- In the last years of his life, King faced mounting criticism from young African American activists who favoured a more confrontational approach to seeking change.

- King and other SCLC members were called to Memphis, Tennessee, to support a sanitation workers' strike.

- While in Memphis, King was assassinated on 4 April 1968.

- His assassination led to an outpouring of anger among black Americans and led to major riots in 100 cities, as well as a period of national mourning, which helped speed the way for the passing of the 1968 Civil Rights Act.

4.5 The extent of progress in civil rights by 1975

- By 1975, there was much greater federal government intervention on civil rights. The 1970 Voting Rights Act banned state literacy tests and the Act was revised in 1975 to include other racial minorities too.

- President Nixon showed limited support to the civil rights movement, but did encourage black businesses and home ownership.

Key terms

National Advisory Commission on Civil Disorders Set up by President Johnson in 1967 following the riots, it asked: What happened? Why did it happen? What can be done to prevent it from happening again and again?

Communist Someone who promotes a classless society where power is shared and private ownership is abolished

Key individuals

Otto Kerner Governor of Illinois from 1961 to 1968

Richard Daley Mayor of Chicago from 1955 to 1976

Revision task

Summarise, in no more than ten words, the contents of the Kerner Report.

Exam tip

Make sure you are able to explain why the civil rights campaign was less prominent after 1968.

- Progress on integration had been made – by 1974, only 8 per cent of black children in the South attended segregated schools.
- However, by 1975 the fight for equality for black Americans was far from won.

 ## RAG: Rate the timeline

Below are an exam-style question and a timeline. Read the question, study the timeline and, using three coloured pens, put a **red**, **amber** or **green** star next to the events to show:

Red: events and policies that have **no** relevance to the question

Amber: events and policies that have **some** relevance to the question

Green: events and policies that have **direct** relevance to the question.

> You may use the following in your answer:
> - The riots of 1965–67
> - Federal action
>
> You **must** also use information of your own.

Explain why there had been some progress made in civil rights in the years 1965–75.

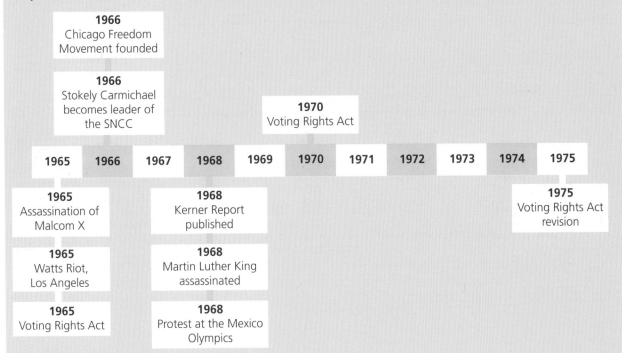

1966 Chicago Freedom Movement founded

1966 Stokely Carmichael becomes leader of the SNCC

1970 Voting Rights Act

| 1965 | 1966 | 1967 | 1968 | 1969 | 1970 | 1971 | 1972 | 1973 | 1974 | 1975 |

1965 Assassination of Malcom X

1968 Kerner Report published

1975 Voting Rights Act revision

1965 Watts Riot, Los Angeles

1968 Martin Luther King assassinated

1965 Voting Rights Act

1968 Protest at the Mexico Olympics

 ## Spot the mistakes

Below is a paragraph which is part of an answer to the question in the timeline activity above. However, it has factual mistakes. Identify the mistakes and, on a separate piece of paper, rewrite the paragraph.

One reason why there was some progress made in civil rights from 1965 to 1975 was the riots of 1965–67 in which ghettos all across America erupted in violence. The riots began in Watts, Chicago in 1965. The riots were a response to army violence and ghetto conditions. Riots continued in the summer months in different cities, mainly in the South. In response, the Kerner Report was published which investigated the causes of the riots. The report was the findings of the National Advisory Commission on Civil Disorders appointed by President Kennedy. It highlighted poor living conditions in the ghettos and the extent to which white racism contributed considerably to the riots. This helped to raise awareness of black American civil rights in the North, which led to Martin Luther King and the SCLC redirecting their campaign from the South.

Key topic 3: US involvement in the Vietnam War, 1954–75

The Vietnam War casts a huge shadow over twentieth-century American history. To understand its impact, it is vital to know the nature of and reasons for US involvement in Vietnam and the tactics used by both sides in the conflict.

1 Reasons for US involvement in Vietnam, 1954–63

REVISED ☐

1.1 The battle of Dien Bien Phu and the end of French rule in Vietnam

- Since the nineteenth century, Vietnam (part of what at the time was called **Indo-China**) had been a French **colony**.
- During the Second World War, Japan took control of Vietnam.
- In 1941, **Ho Chi Minh** helped to set up the **Vietminh** to fight for an independent Vietnam.
- When Japan was defeated in the Second World War, France wanted to restore control over Indo-China. Nine years of war followed between France and the Vietminh.
- In 1954, France suffered a humiliating defeat at the battle of Dien Bien Phu. An **armistice** was signed and France agreed to leave Indo-China.

1.2 Reasons for greater US involvement under Eisenhower

Geneva Agreement

- In May 1954, an agreement was made in Geneva, Switzerland between representatives from Vietnam, France, China, the USSR, USA and Britain to resolve the problem of Vietnam.
- It decided that:
  ○ the withdrawal of France from Vietnam would be formally recognised
  ○ Vietnam would be temporarily divided along the 17th parallel into North and South Vietnam
  ○ the North would be under Vietminh control, led by Ho Chi Minh, while the anti-communist **Ngo Dinh Diem** would lead the South
  ○ democratic elections would be held within two years to reunite Vietnam.
- The USA rejected the Geneva Agreement as it feared a Ho Chi Minh election victory would lead to Vietnam becoming a communist state. Instead it gave military and financial support to Diem's government.

Diem's government

- Diem was an unpopular and ineffectual leader and his government was seen as corrupt, brutal and harsh.
- The USA promoted Diem as he led an anti-Communist South Vietnamese government.
- In total, $1.6 billion in American aid was sent to Vietnam between 1954 and 1960. Military 'advisers' were also sent to help the South Vietnamese army.
- In 1960, the National Liberation Front (NLF), formed by the Vietminh and supported by Ho Chi Minh, was set up to fight against Diem. It began a **guerrilla campaign** against Diem's regime. The NLF was also known as the **Vietcong**.

Key terms

Indo-China Region of Southeast Asia which included Vietnam, Cambodia and Laos

Colony Country or area under political control of another country

Vietminh A nationalist movement set up in 1941, originally to fight for Vietnamese independence from French rule

Armistice Agreement to end hostilities in war

Guerrilla campaign Fighting in small groups against conventional forces

Vietcong Communist-led guerrilla army and political movement

Containment Prevention of communism spreading to non-communist nations

Cold War An ideological conflict from 1945 between the USA and the Soviet Union

Strategic Hamlet Programme US attempt to win over the peasants by moving them into new villages in areas under the control of the South Vietnamese army

CIA (Central Intelligence Agency) US foreign intelligence service

---

Domino theory

- In the 1950s, the USA adopted a policy of **containment**.
- In the context of the **Cold War**, President Eisenhower was determined to prevent the spread of communism to South Vietnam. He was convinced that China and the USSR were planning to spread communism throughout Asia.
- The US government feared that if Vietnam became communist, other countries in Southeast Asia would follow (just like a row of dominoes).

1.3 Greater involvement under Kennedy

- President **John F Kennedy** was determined to be seen to be tough on communism.
- He increased the levels of economic support and military advisers training the South Vietnamese Army (ARVN) to help support Diem's regime. By 1963, there were 16,000 military 'advisers' in Vietnam (there were 800 military advisers in South Vietnam when Kennedy became President in 1961).
- Kennedy inherited the **Strategic Hamlet Programme**. It was led by Diem's government and the **CIA (Central Intelligence Agency)** and was designed to prevent the Vietcong gaining influence over peasants in South Vietnam. This increased the hostility of the peasants towards Diem's government.
- Diem became increasingly unpopular and in November 1963 he was arrested and shot by his own troops in a *coup d'etat*.

> **Exam tip**
>
> You need to know the weaknesses of the Diem government, and why it was necessary for the USA to support it.

> **Key individuals**
>
> **Ho Chi Minh** Joint founder of the Vietminh and President of North Vietnam from 1954 until his death
>
> **Ngo Dinh Diem** Leader of South Vietnam from 1955 until his assassination in 1963
>
> **John F Kennedy** US President from 1961 until his assassination in 1963

> **Revision task**
>
> Create a timeline showing the main developments in US involvement in Vietnam by 1963, adding in dates and events.

 RAG: Rate the timeline

Below are an exam-style question and a timeline. Read the question, study the timeline and, using three coloured pens, put a **red**, amber or green star next to the events to show:

Red: events and policies that have **no** relevance to the question
Amber: events and policies that have **some** relevance to the question
Green: events and policies that have **direct** relevance to the question.

Explain why President Eisenhower became involved in Vietnam.

> You may use the following in your answer:
> - Domino theory
> - Diem's unpopularity
>
> You **must** also use information of your own.

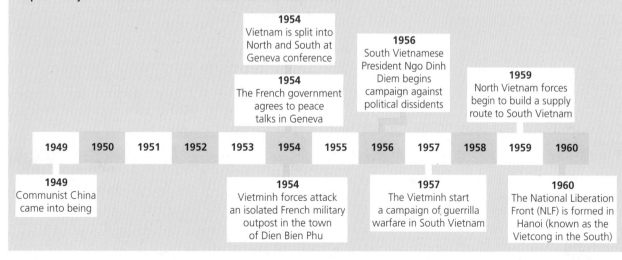

2 Escalation of the conflict under Johnson

US involvement in Vietnam peaked under President **Lyndon B Johnson**. It was clear that there would need to be much more direct US action if the Vietcong was going to be defeated. Johnson would need to convince Congress and US public opinion of the necessity of such action.

2.1 The increasing threat of the Vietcong

- The Vietcong increasingly gained support and control. By the end of 1964, 35 per cent of South Vietnam was controlled by the Vietcong. They were supported by tens of thousands of guerrilla groups operating in South Vietnam.

- The Vietcong was able to score propaganda victories by presenting South Vietnam as a weak American puppet government. The Vietcong supported its troops in South Vietnam by a supply line called the Ho Chi Minh Trail.

- The **ARVN** remained unsuccessful and relied on President Johnson for support.

2.2 The Gulf of Tonkin incident

- On 2 August 1964, North Vietnamese torpedo boats opened fire on US ships in the **Gulf of Tonkin**. The US destroyer attacked was the USS *Maddox* which was gathering intelligence information.

- President Johnson was outraged by this attack and used it as an opportunity to persuade Congress to support even greater US involvement in Vietnam.

- On 7 August, Congress passed the Gulf of Tonkin **Resolution**, which gave the President the power to 'take all necessary measures to prevent further aggression and achieve peace and security'.

- The Resolution escalated the war in Vietnam by effectively granting President Johnson political support to take direct military action against North Vietnam. George Ball, Under-Secretary of State, in a White House meeting in July 1965 said the decision to escalate the war was 'the greatest single error that America has made in its national history'.

2.3 Increased US involvement in Vietnam

- The Gulf of Tonkin Resolution was initially used to increase air support and attacks. After more Vietcong attacks, Johnson approved a massive and regular bombing campaign against North Vietnam called Operation Rolling Thunder. Launched on 7 February 1965, it lasted until 1968.

- The bombing raids were targeted at military and industrial areas in North Vietnam. Operation Rolling Thunder was intended to put military pressure on North Vietnam's communist leaders and reduce their capacity to wage war against the government of South Vietnam.

- Over 1 million tons of bombs dropped on Vietnam. Between 1965 and 1973, three times as many bombs dropped on Vietnam as had fallen on Europe, Asia and Africa during the Second World War.

- To support the bombing campaign, Johnson sent American ground troops into Vietnam. By the end of 1965, 200,000 ground troops were in Vietnam, increasing to 586,000 by 1968.

Key terms

ARVN The army of the Republic of South Vietnam

Gulf of Tonkin A body of water located off the coast of northern Vietnam and southern China

Resolution A formal decision taken at a meeting by means of a vote

Key individual

Lyndon B Johnson President Kennedy's vice-president, who succeeded him as President of the USA from 1963 to 1969

Revision task

Make a table to show reasons for the increasing threat of the Vietcong, using these headings:

- Guerrilla campaigns
- Ho Chi Minh Trail
- Weakness of the ARVN

Exam tip

Be aware of the details of the Gulf of Tonkin incident and how it led to increased US involvement in Vietnam.

You're the examiner

1 Below are an exam-style question, a mark scheme and a paragraph written in answer to the question. Read the paragraph and the mark scheme and decide what mark you would give the answer.

Give two things you can infer from Source A about President Johnson's reaction to the Gulf of Tonkin incident. (4 marks)

SOURCE A

From a speech by President Johnson to the American people, 4 August 1964.

The performance of commanders and crews in this engagement is in the highest tradition of the United States Navy. But repeated acts of violence against the Armed Forces of the United States must be met not only with alert defense, but with positive reply. That reply is being given as I speak to you tonight. Air action is now in execution against gunboats and certain supporting facilities in North Vietnam, which have been used in these hostile operations.

Mark scheme	
2 marks	1 mark for each valid inference up to a maximum of two inferences
2 marks	The second mark for each inference is for supporting detail selected from the source

STUDENT ANSWER

The source suggests that America is responding to North Vietnamese violence. The source also suggests that America deployed air attacks against North Vietnam in response to the Gulf of Tonkin incident.

Mark ☐ Reason _____

_____

2 Now write an answer which could gain four marks.

 Concentric circles

In the concentric circles, rank order the following reasons for increased US involvement in Vietnam, beginning with the most important in the middle to the least important on the outside. Explain your decisions.

- French withdrawal
- The domino theory
- Weaknesses of Diem's government
- Increasing threat of the Vietcong
- The Gulf of Tonkin incident

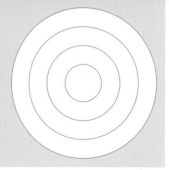

3 The nature of the conflict in Vietnam, 1964–68, Part 1 REVISED ☐

The conflict in Vietnam was a struggle between two completely different methods of warfare.

3.1 Guerrilla tactics used by the Vietcong

- The Vietcong was much less armed against the combined forces of the US military and the ARVN. It had around 170,000 soldiers, and they would be no match for the US army in traditional combat. Ho Chi Minh believed that superior forces could be defeated by guerrilla tactics and had successfully used these tactics previously against Japan and France.
- Guerrilla tactics were based on simple principles: retreat when the enemy attacks; raid when the enemy camps; attack when the enemy tires; pursue when the enemy retreats. The Vietcong would not confront their enemy in an all-out, open battle. Instead, they would frustrate their opponents, inflict enough damage to make the war unpopular with the US public so that US forces would have to withdraw and wear down the morale of the ARVN.
- This approach relied on support from the peasants in South Vietnam, who hid the Vietcong and passed on their vast knowledge and understanding of the jungles of South Vietnam.

How effective were the guerrilla tactics?

- The US army found the guerrilla tactics extremely difficult to fight against.
- As the Vietcong did not wear uniform, they were almost impossible to identify. After they attacked, they would disappear into the jungle and villages, but the US army could not trace them as they were indistinguishable from the local peasants.
- This meant that the US soldiers lived in constant fear of an **ambush**. Around 11 per cent of US deaths were caused by **booby traps**, increasing **psychological** fear and damaging US army morale.
- The use of guerrilla tactics helped to promote the mental strength of the Vietcong; they refused to give in.
- The Ho Chi Minh Trail ensured that there were supplies and replacement troops available and the Vietcong worked hard to maintain the support of the local population.
- The Vietcong treated the South Vietnamese peasants with respect and even helped them in the fields. In return, many peasants helped the Vietcong by keeping them safe and the Ho Chi Minh Trail open.
- The Vietcong could also be ruthless and brutal in punishing peasants who opposed them. Between 1966 and 1971, the Vietcong killed an estimated 30,000 civilians who worked for the South Vietnamese government.

Tunnels

- The Vietminh had successfully used tunnels to transport and protect their soldiers in the war against France.
- The Vietcong developed this system by digging deep tunnels and using them as air raid shelters to protect them from US bombing raids, such as the **Cu Chi Tunnels**.
- Some tunnels contained hospitals, storage areas and living spaces to house and protect guerrilla fighters.
- The tunnels were very narrow and hard for the US army to locate. The Vietnamese people were often smaller than most Americans, so many of the tunnels were much too small for most US troops to enter. The Vietcong sometimes protected them with booby traps.

Key terms

Ambush A surprise attack

Booby trap A device that is intended to kill, harm or surprise a person

Psychological Affecting the mind

Cu Chi Tunnels A network of connecting underground tunnels located around Saigon

Revision task

Summarise the tunnel system in no more than ten words.

Exam tip

Make sure you are aware of the countries which helped support the Ho Chi Minh Trail.

How important

On a separate piece of paper, copy out and complete the table below.

● Briefly summarise why each tactic helped the Vietcong in the Vietnam War.
● Make a decision about the importance of each factor in helping the Vietcong to try to secure victory. Give a brief explanation for each choice.

Factor	Key features	Decisive/important/quite important
Ho Chi Minh Trail		
Winning the support of the South Vietnamese peasants		
Vietcong Tunnels		
Dressing like ordinary Vietnamese people		
Ambushes and booby traps		
Using light weapons and equipment		

Utility

Below are a utility question and an answer focusing on the utility of the contents of the source. On a separate piece of paper complete the answer by explaining the utility of the nature, origins and purpose of the source. You could look at page 43 for guidance on how to answer the utility question to help you make your judgement.

How useful is Source A for an enquiry into the tactics of the Vietcong in the Vietnam War? Explain your answer, using Source A and your knowledge of the historical context.

SOURCE A

Extracts from a letter written in 1965 by Lê Duẩn, secretary of the North Vietnamese Communist Party and one of Ho Chi Minh's closest associates. The letter explains how North Vietnam was planning to react to the large-scale arrival of US forces in 1965.

We must not neglect the political war. I just talked about the possibility and necessity to strengthen the political war. Even though the US brings in more troops to Vietnam, they will fail to weaken our political power. In fact, our political power is likely to be enhanced and the US will be isolated and fail miserably. The more troops the US brings in, the more military bases it builds, the larger area it occupies, the more sophisticated weapons it uses, the more B.52 bombs it drops, the more chemical poisons it uses, the worse the conflict between our people and them becomes, the more our people hate them.

Source A is useful for an enquiry into tactics of the Vietcong in the Vietnam War because it suggests that the Vietcong guerrilla tactics will be more effective than the traditional tactics employed by the US Army. This is shown in the source by reference to the acknowledgement that 'even though the US brings in more troops to Vietnam, they will fail to weaken our political power'. This is supported by my knowledge of the tactics of the Vietcong. They were prepared to fight for as long as it took to win a united Vietnam. They used propaganda and gave talks to the villages in South Vietnam about their cause. Some Vietcong fighters even lived in the villages and helped to work on the land. By integrating themselves with the rural population in this way, they ensured the peasants were supportive of the Vietcong and their tactics.

Source A is also useful because ...

3 The nature of the conflict in Vietnam, 1964–68, Part 2

3.2 Methods used by the USA

US military tactics were designed to attack North Vietnam and defend South Vietnam. These tactics were based on the use of superior military force. Despite these great efforts, the communist forces remained undefeated.

Chemical weapons

● The US decided to use **defoliants** to destroy the jungle. This would make it easier for US forces to locate the Vietcong bases and remove the Vietcong food supplies.

● The first chemical weapon sprayed was in August 1961; 24 per cent of South Vietnam was sprayed with chemical weapons between 1964 and 1970.

● Agent Orange, a highly toxic weedkiller, was used on the jungle forests. Its purpose was to destroy the jungle where the Vietcong hid. The US used around 77 million litres of Agent Orange, wiping out 4 million acres of forests and farms. An estimated 4 million Vietnamese people were exposed to it.

● **Napalm** was another widely-used chemical weapon. Around 400,000 tons of napalm were dropped between 1965 and 1973.

● The air attacks were not very accurate. Many South Vietnamese civilians and soldiers were also killed by these chemical weapons.

● The poison stayed in the soil and affected crops for decades afterwards. Many Vietnamese children were born with health defects.

Search and Destroy

● The policy of Search and Destroy was developed by US Commander **General William Westmoreland**.

● It involved establishing heavily defended US bases in South Vietnam, then launching raids on Vietcong villages by helicopter to destroy hideouts and discover weapons stores.

● The troops called these attacks 'Zippos' raids (this was in reference to the name of the cigarette lighters they used to set fire to villages).

● The raids were effective in locating and destroying Vietcong strategic locations.

● However, inexperienced US troops often walked into traps set by the Vietcong and civilian casualties were extremely high in these raids, which made the US and South Vietnamese forces very unpopular with the peasants and increased their support for the Vietcong.

3.3 The Tet Offensive, 1968

● The Vietcong had planned a series of surprise attacks in over 100 towns, cities and military targets in the South during the **Tet** public holiday in January 1968.

● There was normally a **ceasefire** during this period, so many ARVN were on leave.

● The Vietcong believed their offensive would increase support from people in the South, as well as appeal to US public opinion to reduce US involvement in the conflict.

● One Vietcong unit tried to capture the US embassy in Saigon, which was shown live on US television.

Key terms

Defoliant A chemical that removes the leaves from trees and plants, used in warfare

Napalm A highly flammable sticky jelly used in incendiary bombs

Tet Vietnamese New Year, the most important celebration in Vietnamese culture

Ceasefire A temporary stoppage of a war

Key individual

General William Westmoreland United States Army general, who commanded US forces during the Vietnam War from 1964 to 1968

Revision task

Compare the Tet Offensive with the Gulf of Tonkin Incident – look for similarities and differences on the effect both events had on US involvement in Vietnam.

Exam tip

Ensure you have precise knowledge of the details of the Tet Offensive and can explain the impact it had on US public opinion about the Vietnam War.

- The Vietcong captured the ancient city of Hué. They held it for 25 days before it was captured by US and ARVN forces. Hué was destroyed in the process.

- The Vietcong lost around 10,000 troops in the Tet Offensive and was badly weakened by it. Very few people in the South joined them.

- However, the Tet Offensive is seen as a turning point in the war as it provoked a growing feeling in the USA that the war was unwinnable and ignited a huge rise in opposition to the war.

 ## Complete the paragraph

Below are an exam-style question and a paragraph which is part of the answer to the question. The paragraph contains a limited amount of detail. Annotate the paragraph to add additional detail to the answer.

Study Interpretations 1 and 2. They give different views on the consequences of Operation Rolling Thunder. What is the main difference between the views? Explain your answer, using details from both interpretations.

INTERPRETATION 1

From United States 1776–1992 *by Derrick Murphy, Kathryn Cooper and Mark Waldron, published in 2001.*

The desire to close down the Ho Chi Minh Trail led to Operation Rolling Thunder. Although between 1965 and 1968 more bombs were dropped on North Vietnam than all the bombs dropped in the Second World War, they failed to have a significant effect. In the cities of North Vietnam production was moved out of Hanoi and spread around the country so that the raids did minimal damage. On the Trail, the North Vietnamese and Vietcong simply built another road in another part of the jungle.

INTERPRETATION 2

From Access to History Context: An Introduction to American History 1860–1990 *by Alan Farmer and Vivienne Sanders, published in 2002.*

Operation Rolling Thunder ... was very expensive ... in 1964 the war cost the US tax-payer under half a billion dollars ... in 1968 it cost $26.5 billion. The war was the main contributor to the government's $25 billion deficit and to rising inflation in 1968. The Treasury warning that the war could not go on, coupled with tax-payer resentment, helped convince Johnson that the escalation must stop and Nixon that the war must end.

A main difference is that Interpretation 1 emphasises the military impact of Operation Rolling Thunder. Interpretation 2 does not.

4 Changes under Nixon, 1969–73

4.1 The Nixon Doctrine

- President **Richard Nixon**, campaigning to become President in 1968 at a time when the war was increasingly unpopular in the USA, promised the war in Vietnam would continue until 'peace with honour' could be achieved. His aim was to withdraw the USA from the war as soon as possible, while still leaving the South Vietnam regime in power.
- On 25 July 1969 President Nixon advanced his views about the role of the USA in Southeast Asia. This became known as the Nixon **Doctrine**. He assured America's friends in Asia that 'We will keep our treaty commitments.' This meant that the USA would honour its current defence commitments. He also promised to support any ally against a nuclear threat.
- However, Nixon also made clear that the USA would not commit troops in any new conflict. Instead, it would provide aid and military advice, with the expectation that the country under threat would provide its own troops.

4.2 Vietnamisation

- The Nixon Doctrine led to a policy of **Vietnamisation**. It was introduced to fulfil Nixon's electoral promise to end the war in Vietnam and to **pacify** increasing US opposition to the war.
- The USA would continue to provide economic and military aid and support to the ARVN. By strengthening South Vietnamese forces so that they could defend themselves, the USA would withdraw its own troops without appearing to have been defeated.
- Vietnamisation started in 1969. The strategy had limited success. By the end of 1969, 60,000 troops had been withdrawn. This was a move welcomed by most US citizens, because there were fewer US troops in Vietnam and, consequently, fewer casualties. However, without US support, the ARVN was no match for the communist forces.

4.3 Attacks on Cambodia, Laos and North Vietnam

- Nixon ordered a massive increase in bombing to try to convince the North to look for peace.
- Cambodia – a **neutral** country – was subjected to heavy bombing in order to attack the Vietcong safe havens outside of Vietnam. The Ho Chi Minh Trail, which extended into Cambodia, was also targeted in order to try to cut off the Vietcong supply lines.
- The Cambodian campaign shocked both US Congress and US public opinion because Nixon was supposed to be stopping the war, not extending it.
- In February 1971, the USA gave air support for the South Vietnamese invasion of Laos.
- Nixon also ordered increased air raids over North Vietnam after 1971 to try to further weaken it. This continued in April 1972 with the launch of Operation Linebacker II. Both Hanoi and Haiphong were bombed, with Haiphong harbour attacked to prevent ships from China and the USSR reaching North Vietnam.
- The bombing of North Vietnam further escalated in the autumn of 1972 to try to win concessions from the communists at peace talks in Paris. The *New York Times* called the bombing 'Diplomacy through terror'.

Key terms

Doctrine A stated set of beliefs held by an individual or group

Vietnamisation Nixon's policy to train and equip the South Vietnamese soldiers to take the place of US troops

Pacify To reduce anger and bring peace to a situation

Neutral Not supporting or helping either side in a conflict

Key individual

Richard Nixon US president from 1969 until his resignation in 1974

Revision task

Create a table to show the strengths and weaknesses of the policy of Vietnamisation.

Exam tip

You need to be aware of the motivation and impact of Nixon's attacks on Cambodia, Laos and North Vietnam.

Organising knowledge

Use the information on pages 22–30 to complete the table below to summarise the key changes in attitudes to Vietnam under each US president.

	Attitudes	Actions
President Eisenhower		
President Kennedy		
President Johnson		
President Nixon		

Making an inference from a visual source

An inference is a message that you can get from a source by reading between the lines. Below are an exam-style inference question, the source and a series of statements. Decide which of the statements:

- make(s) inferences from the source (I)
- describes what it can see in the source (D)
- cannot be justified from the source (X).

Give two things you can infer from Source A about the policy of Vietnamisation.

SOURCE A

A US cartoon, published in 1972. The crows represent the communist forces.

Statement	I	D	X
The cartoon shows a scarecrow in tatters as it is being attacked by communist forces			
The American policy of Vietnamisation is in tatters			
South Vietnam could not win the war on its own			
America could not surrender because since 1965 the US government had been telling people at home that the war was just and vital			
Nixon came to power in 1968 with the intention of ending the war in Vietnam			
Nixon decided to put more of the burden of war on the shoulders of the government of South Vietnam, requiring them to do more of the fighting so US troops could be withdrawn			
Once the ARVN no longer had direct US military support, the Vietcong became far more superior			

Key topic 4: Reactions to, and the end of, US involvement in Vietnam, 1964–75

The Vietnam War became a divisive issue in American society. Opposition to the war, encouraged by the media, increased in momentum after 1968. In 1973, peace talks were completed that led to the withdrawal of US support. Within two years the Communists had taken control of the whole country.

1 Opposition to the war

1.1 Reasons for the growth of opposition

Although some anti-war groups disapproved from the start, before 1964 there was broad support for US involvement in Vietnam from across US society. However, once President Johnson escalated US military involvement during 1965–68, opposition to the war grew.

The student movement

Many (but not all) students felt that the Vietnam War was an abuse of the government's power and protested against the conflict. Many students held **sit-ins**, **boycotts**, demonstrations and protests (which sometimes involved burning the US flag). Anti-war protestors launched a campaign against the conscription of young men into the army. Many students burnt their **draft** cards. There were many student slogans against the war in Vietnam, including, 'Hey! Hey! LBJ [President Lyndon B Johnson], How many kids did you kill today?'

TV and media coverage of the war

The Vietnam War was the first to be televised and so was in the 'living rooms' of most US families. News reports regularly showed the appalling injuries sustained in the war, especially the use of napalm against innocent civilians, often women and young children. Well-respected TV reporters, such as **Walter Cronkite** of CBS News publicly suggested that the Vietnam War was unwinnable. The media reported the large-scale anti-war protests that were spreading across the USA.

The draft system

Conscription had existed since the Second World War. It was compulsory for men aged 18–35 to serve a period of time in the military forces. Exemptions often favoured the wealthy, so a much higher proportion of black and working-class Americans were called up. One high profile African American boxer, Muhammed Ali, refused to obey the draft – he was stripped of his world title and authorities removed his passport. The Draft Resistance Movement was formed, giving advice on how to avoid conscription, while some men also fled to Canada or joined universities.

1.2 Public reaction to the My Lai Massacre, 1968 and the trial of Lt Calley

The My Lai Massacre

On 16 March 1968, a patrol of US soldiers carried out a 'Search and Destroy' mission in the village of My Lai in South Vietnam. The village was wiped out, with around 400 civilians killed. No Vietcong were found. The massacre was kept a secret until a soldier gave an account of it to the US media in late 1969. It caused public outrage, fuelled the anti-war movement and undermined the war effort.

The trial of Lt Calley

An official investigation into the My Lai Massacre was launched. The soldiers in charge of the My Lai operation were put on trial for mass murder. Only Lieutenant Calley was found guilty and in 1971 he was given a 20-year prison sentence, although he was released in 1974.

Key terms

Sit-in A form of direct action that involves one or more people occupying an area in protest

Boycott To withdraw from commercial or social relations as a form of punishment or protest

Draft US name for conscription, compulsory for men over the age of 18

Key individual

Walter Cronkite Respected TV journalist from CBS News who reported from Vietnam

---

1.3 The Kent State University shootings, 1970

In 1970, President Nixon ordered the invasion of Cambodia and this increased demonstrations against the war (which by now often ended in violent clashes with the police). In 1970, US National Guards opened fire on a large group of anti-war protestors at Kent State University in Ohio. Four people were killed and eleven injured. The public was shocked. Students went on strike in protest at the action and there was worldwide press coverage of the event.

Exam tip

You need to be aware of the impact of the media on the US government at this time, in terms of informing the population and influencing policy-making decisions.

 You're the examiner

1 Below are an exam-style question, a mark scheme and a paragraph which is part of an answer to the question. Read the paragraph and the mark scheme. Decide which level you would award the paragraph. Write the level below, along with a justification for your choice.

Explain why the Vietnam War became unpopular in the USA.

You may use the following in your answer:
- The role of the media
- Student protests

You must also use information of your own.

Mark scheme		
Level	**Mark**	
1	1–3	A simple or generalised answer is given, lacking development and organisation
2	4–6	An explanation is given, showing limited analysis and with only an implicit link to the question
3	7–9	An explanation is given, showing some analysis, which is mainly directed at the focus of the question
4	10–12	An analytical explanation is given which is directed consistently at the focus of the question

STUDENT ANSWER

A reason why the Vietnam War became unpopular in the USA was because of the media coverage of the war. The American press and TV news were often accused of undermining the American government in its effort to win in Vietnam. Reports often showed graphic and shocking violence and this served to horrify the American public about the nature of the war their country was fighting. Very well-respected TV reporters, such as Walter Cronkite of CBS News for example, publicly suggested that the Vietnam War was unwinnable. This had a significant effect on shifting American public opinion against the war effort.

Remember that for the higher levels, students must:
- explain at least three reasons
- focus explicitly on the question
- support their reasons with precise details.

Mark ☐ Reason _____

2 Now suggest what the student has to do to achieve a higher level.

_____

3 Try and rewrite this paragraph at a higher level.
4 Now try and write the rest of the answer to the question.

Key topic 4: Reactions to, and the end of, US involvement in Vietnam, 1964–75

2 Support for the war

A wide range of people across US society **patriotically** and enthusiastically supported the Vietnam War. In a 1964 poll, 85 per cent of Americans supported US government policy on the war.

2.1 Reasons for support for the war, including the fear of communism

- Fear of communism was very strong and was heightened by the establishment of communism in China in 1949 under **Mao Zedong**, the expansion of communism in Eastern Europe by the Soviet Union and the '**Red Scare**' in US society.
- There was widespread fear of the domino theory – if Vietnam fell to communism, it would be followed by other countries in Southeast Asia in quick succession, something the USA wished to avoid.
- In the early years of the war, the media largely followed official policy for fear of being accused of undermining the war effort.

2.2 The 'hard hats' and the 'silent majority'

The 'hard hats'

- The American people were fiercely patriotic and were committed to defend South Vietnam in order to protect America's national honour.
- Once involved in the conflict, they did not want the USA to 'lose face' by withdrawing from the war and see its power and influence in the world diminished.
- 'Hard hats' was the name given to the construction workers who actively supported the Vietnam War and demonstrated against the anti-war protestors, sometimes by force. This was best seen in the Hard Hat riot of May 1970 in New York.
- President Nixon claimed the hard hats were supporters of 'freedom and patriotism'.

The 'silent majority'

- On 3 November 1969, President Nixon appealed for the support of 'the great silent majority' in a televised speech about US policy in Vietnam.
- Nixon believed these were Americans who supported his policies but did not actively campaign or participate in the war demonstrations.
- A poll carried out after this speech showed that 77 per cent of people supported President Nixon's policy in Vietnam.
- This result ensured President Nixon received support from Congress and enabled him to proceed with an exit from Vietnam which secured an 'honourable peace'.

Key terms

Patriotically Expressing strong support for your country

Red Scare Term used in the USA involving promotion of a widespread fear that immigrants from Eastern Europe would bring about a rise in communism in the USA

Key individual

Mao Zedong Commonly known as Chairman Mao, he was a Chinese communist revolutionary who became the founding father of the People's Republic of China from 1949

Revision task

List the main reasons why people supported the war in Vietnam. Put an arrow beside each to indicate whether this support would have changed as the war progressed.

Exam tip

Remember to give a balanced evaluation of US public opinion towards the Vietnam War. It is vital to recall the considerable support given to the war, when referring to the public opposition of it.

You're the examiner

1 Below are an exam-style question, a mark scheme and a paragraph written in answer to the question. Read the paragraph and the mark scheme and decide what mark you would give the answer.

Give two things you can infer from Source A about reasons why the USA was involved in Vietnam.

SOURCE A

From a speech by the US Vice-President, Richard Nixon, in December 1953.

If Indo-China falls, Thailand is put in an almost impossible position. The same is true of Malaya with its rubber and tin. The same is true of Indonesia. If this whole part of Southeast Asia goes under communist domination or communist influence, Japan, who trades and must trade with this area in order to exist must inevitably be oriented towards the communist regime.

Mark scheme	
2 marks	1 mark for each valid inference up to a maximum of two inferences
2 marks	The second mark for each inference is for supporting detail selected from the source

STUDENT ANSWER

The source suggests that communism will spread into other areas. The source also suggests that American trade with Japan will be at risk.

Mark ☐ Reason _____

_____

2 Now write an answer which could gain four marks.

 Concentric circles

In the concentric circles, rank order the following reasons for support for the war in Vietnam, beginning with the most important in the middle to the least important on the outside. Explain your decisions.

- The domino theory
- Fear of communism
- Defending national pride
- Commitment to South Vietnam

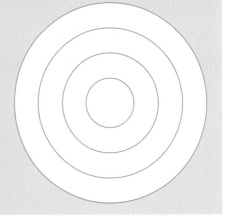

3 The peace process and end of the war

With no victory in sight, growing casualties and increasing costs, the motivation for peace was desirable for both sides involved in the Vietnam War.

3.1 Reasons for, and features of, the peace negotiations, 1972–73

- The Tet Offensive triggered initial talks to secure a peace deal in Vietnam. These were held in Paris in 1968. However, no progress was made.
- Major issues prevented an agreement being reached. These included the reunification of Vietnam, the nature of how South Vietnam was to be governed and the withdrawal of US troops from South Vietnam.
- President Nixon wanted to end the war as quickly as possible and took a number of steps to try to achieve that:
  - Nixon held talks with China and the USSR and a period of improved relations in the Cold War known as *détente* was established. North Vietnam feared a possible loss of aid from USSR and China as a result.
  - He pursued his Vietnamisation policy of reducing troop numbers in Vietnam – by 1972 there were only 24,200 troops (compared to 543,000 in 1969). US troops were replaced by an increase in the numbers in the ARVN.
  - Nixon authorised **Henry Kissinger**, the US National Security Advisor, to open secret negotiations with North Vietnam.
  - He escalated the bombing raids in North Vietnam and also raids to destroy the Ho Chi Minh Trail – this included bombing Cambodia, where he also sent ground troops in April 1970.

3.2 The significance of the Paris Peace Agreement, 1973

- In January 1973, a ceasefire was signed in Paris. On 27 January 1973, a formal agreement was signed and the Vietnam War was over.
- The Paris Peace Accords, as they became known, pledged to 'respect the independence, **sovereignty**, unity and territorial integrity of Vietnam as recognised by the 1954 Geneva Agreements on Vietnam'.
- US troops were to be withdrawn within 60 days. The agreement ended US involvement in Vietnam.
- The agreement failed to secure the future of an independent non-communist South Vietnam as the civil war in Vietnam continued. Without US support, the economy of South Vietnam crashed and when the ceasefire ended in 1974, the ARVN could not withstand the pressure of the Vietcong. After the fall of Saigon in 1975 (which was then renamed Ho Chi Minh City), North and South Vietnam merged on 2 July 1976 to form the Socialist Republic of Vietnam.

3.3 The economic and human costs of the war for the USA

- US involvement in Vietnam was very expensive, costing around $167 billion.
- There were 58,183 American deaths and a further 300,000 were wounded.
- Returning soldiers found it hard to cope with what they had experienced. Many found it hard to secure employment and there were high rates of suicide among veterans of the war as they struggled to deal with post-traumatic stress.
- A lack of trust emerged between the government and the people. Many politicians felt the USA should be more careful not to get involved in conflicts with other countries as there was a realisation that there were limits to US power.

Key terms

Détente A period in the 1970s when Cold War relations between the USA and the USSR appeared to be more relaxed

Sovereignty The authority of a state to govern itself

Key individual

Henry Kissinger US National Security Advisor and later Secretary of State, he received the Nobel Peace Prize in 1973 for his negotiations which led to the Paris Peace Accords

Revision task

Summarise in no more than ten words the US policy of Vietnamisation.

Exam tip

Remember that President Nixon had promised 'peace with honour' in his presidential election campaign in 1968. Failure to deliver this would cost him electoral support at home.

RAG: Rate the timeline

Below are an exam-style question and a timeline. Read the question, study the timeline and, using three coloured pens, put a **red**, **amber** or **green** star next to the events to show:

Red: events and policies that have **no** relevance to the question

Amber: events and policies that have **some** relevance to the question

Green: events and policies that have **direct** relevance to the question.

Explain why the Paris Peace Agreement was signed in 1973.

You may use the following in your answer:
- Vietnamisation
- Influence of China and USSR

You must also use information of your own.

1969
November My Lai Massacre made public

1970
Nixon orders the bombing of Cambodia

1969
Nixon's policy of Vietnamisation began

1968 January
Tet Offensive

1968	1969	1970	1971	1972	1973

1968 March
My Lai Massacre

1969 July
Secret peace talks held between the USA and North Vietnam

1970
Kent State University shootings

1973 January
Ceasefire agreement is reached in Paris

How important

Complete the table below.

- Briefly summarise why each factor contributed to the ending of the Vietnam War in the years 1968–73.
- Make a decision about the importance of each factor in changing the US and North Vietnamese governments' attitudes to peace. Give a brief explanation for each choice.

Factor	Key features	Decisive/important/quite important
Election of US President Nixon		
Nixon's talks with China and USSR		
US Congress cutting funding		
Increasing US opposition to the war		
Continued heavy bombing of North Vietnam		
Rising costs of the war		
Increasing casualties of the war		
Failure of US tactics		
Vietcong tactics		

4 Reasons for the failure of the USA in Vietnam

The US failure in Vietnam needs to be explained in the context that they were fighting against a committed and experienced guerrilla army, which had advantages that the USA found difficult to match.

4.1 The strengths of North Vietnam

- The North had a good knowledge of the environment and terrain of South Vietnam, as well as a cultural and social understanding of the society they were fighting.
- Many people in North and South Vietnam desired a united and independent Vietnam. Ho Chi Minh successfully portrayed himself as a Vietnamese nationalist.
- The North Vietnam forces successfully instilled a determination in their supporters to reject US foreign intervention and accept the costs of war in order to achieve their war aims.
- The South Vietnam government was unpopular, so it was difficult to present it as an acceptable alternative to communism.

The significance of Russian and Chinese support

- North Vietnam received financial, strategic and moral support from other communist countries.
- China also supported North Vietnam with troops – between 1965 and 1971, over 320,000 troops were sent.
- The USA could never commit to total victory in Vietnam for fear this would lead to direct military intervention by China and USSR and escalate the Cold War.

Vietcong tactics

- The Vietcong's guerrilla tactics were very effective and difficult to undermine using conventional warfare based on superior technology.
- The Vietcong had a clear ideology and were well organised. Bombing raids failed to damage the morale of the North Vietnamese.
- The communist policy of fair land redistribution appealed to the peasants throughout Vietnam.
- The Vietcong enjoyed largely sympathetic support from the local community.

The Ho Chi Minh Trail

- The Ho Chi Minh Trail was a network of hidden forest paths which linked the South to the North.
- The Trail was used to move supplies and troops into South Vietnam.
- The US frequently bombed it but the Vietnamese people worked to keep it open, often enduring terrible conditions.

4.2 The weaknesses of the US armed forces

- The US Army lacked an understanding of Vietnam, and underestimated their enemy.
- Many US troops were young (average age was 19), inexperienced soldiers, who served for one year, which meant camaraderie within units was difficult to establish.
- The conditions were unpleasant as soldiers, many of whom turned to drugs, fought in harsh weather conditions and endured a constant fear of booby traps.
- The war was not supported at home – public opinion, Congress and the media were all hostile to the war. Therefore, as the US public began to oppose the war, military decisions were overtaken by political ones.

Revision task

Draw a timeline of the Vietnam War, including the beginnings of US involvement. On the timeline, highlight the key developments which helped North Vietnam eventually secure victory.

The failure of US tactics

- The US armed forces failed to win the hearts and minds of the Vietnamese people.
- As they could not distinguish the Vietcong from the non-communist Vietnamese, they frequently mistreated South Vietnamese civilians, such as in the My Lai Massacre.
- Bombing raids destroyed South Vietnamese villages, which further alienated many Vietnamese from the ARVN.
- The USA was seen as an imperialist force and was undermined by its support for the unpopular South Vietnam government.

4.3 The impact of opposition to the war in the USA

- As anti-war protests back home in the USA increased, the morale of the US Army declined.
- As troops withdrew as part of President Nixon's Vietnamisation policy, those left behind questioned why they were risking their lives in a conflict that their country did not wholeheartedly support.

Exam tip

The reasons for the failure of the USA in Vietnam are complex. However, you will need a thorough knowledge of how these reasons link together in order to offer a judgement about which reason was the most important and why.

 Relevance

Below are an exam-style question and a series of statements. Decide which statements are:

- relevant to the question (R)
- partially relevant to the question (PR)
- irrelevant to the question (I).

Tick the appropriate column.

Explain why the USA failed in Vietnam.

> You may use the following in your answer:
> - The weakness of the US armed forces
> - The strengths of the Vietcong tactics
>
> You **must** also use information of your own.

Reasons for US failure in Vietnam	R	PR	I
American troops were sent on patrols, to be supported by air and artillery if attacked by the Vietcong. This demoralised soldiers, who realised they were being used as bait to draw out the enemy			
Nixon wanted to ease the tensions of the Cold War and in 1972 he visited China and then the USSR			
The Tet Offensive marked a turning point because it showed the US public that, despite all the bombs, troops and money spent, little was being achieved			
The South Vietnamese government was unpopular and corrupt			
The Vietcong's message of independence from foreign control and ending the concentration of land ownership among rich landlords made it popular with Vietnamese peasant farmers			
The US lacked an understanding of Vietnam's culture, geography and political context to be able to fight the war effectively			
North Vietnam received aid and military support from the USSR and China			
The draft meant that US troops were young and inexperienced and the threat of an invisible enemy and hidden traps had a demoralising psychological impact on US troops			
Vietcong guerrillas were kept well supplied by a constant stream of food and weapons from the North via the Ho Chi Minh Trail			
The Vietcong's guerrilla warfare was more suited to the terrain of the country than US tactics of conventional warfare			
The US bombing campaign failed because the bombs often missed their targets, falling into empty jungle			
The brutal tactics used by US troops often drove more Vietnamese civilians to support the Vietcong			

Exam focus

Your History GCSE is made up of three exams:

- Paper 1 on a thematic study and historic environment
- Paper 2 on a British depth study and a period study
- Paper 3 on a modern depth study, in your case The USA, 1954–75.

For Paper 3 you have to answer the following types of questions. Each requires you to demonstrate different historical skills:

- **Question 1** is a source inference question in which you have to make two supported inferences.
- **Question 2** is a causation question which asks you to explain why something happened. You should develop at least three clear points.
- **Question 3** includes four sub-questions on an enquiry. For this enquiry you are given two sources and two interpretations.

The table below gives a summary of the question types for Paper 3 and what you need to do.

Question number	Marks	Key words	You need to...
1	4	Give **two** things you can infer from Source A about ...	• Make at least two inferences • Use quotes from the source to back up your inference, or describe a specific part of it if it is a picture
2	12	Explain why ... You may use the following in your answer: [two given points] You **must** also use information of your own	• Explain at least three causes. You can use the points in the question but must also use at least one point of your own • Ensure that you focus these on the question
3(a)	8	How useful are sources ... for an enquiry into ...?	• Ensure that you explain the value of the contents of each of the sources • Explain how the provenance of each source affects the value of the contents • You need to support your answer with your knowledge of the given topic
3(b)	4	Study Interpretations 1 and 2. What is the main difference between these views?	• Ensure you understand the main view of each interpretation • Give the view from each interpretation to support your answer
3(c)	4	Suggest **one** reason why Interpretations 1 and 2 give different views	• Remember you only have to explain one reason • Make use of the two sources
3(d)	20	How far do you agree with Interpretation 2 about ...?	• Ensure you agree and disagree with the view • Use evidence from the interpretations and your own knowledge • Ensure you write a conclusion giving your final judgement on the question • There are up to 4 marks for spelling, punctuation, grammar and the use of specialist terminology

Question 1: Inference

Below is an example of an exam-style inference question which is worth 4 marks.

Give two things you can infer from Source A about the Black Power movement.

SOURCE A

Stokely Carmichael explaining Black Power in The New York Review of Books, *22 September 1966.*

We should begin with the basic fact that black Americans have two problems: they are poor and they are black … black Americans are propertyless people in a country where property is valued above all … With power the masses could make or participate in making the decisions which govern their destinies, and thus create basic change in their day-to-day lives.

How to answer

You have to make two inferences and support each with details from the source. For each of the two inferences you are given the prompts 'What I can infer' and 'Details in the source that tell me this'.

- **'What I can infer'** Begin your answer with 'This source suggests …' This should help you to get the message from the source.

- **'Details in the source that tell me this'** Then quote the detail from the source which supports this message. Begin this part of the answer with 'I know this because the source says/shows …'

Below is a sample answer to this inference question with comments alongside it.

What I can infer: The source suggests that the Black Power movement recognises that black Americans live in a worse economic state than white Americans, especially regarding their living conditions.	The first inference is made. Using the phrase 'the source suggests' encourages this inference.
Details in the source that tell me this: I know this because the source says 'black Americans are propertyless people in a country where property is valued above all'.	The first inference is supported with evidence from the source. This is reinforced by using the phrase 'I know this because'.
What I can infer: The source also suggests the Black Power movement is clearly a political movement which hopes to improve the living conditions of black Americans.	The second inference is made. Using the phrase 'the source suggests' encourages this inference.
Details in the source that tell me this: I know this because the source says 'with power the masses could make or participate in making the decisions which govern their destinies'.	The second inference is supported with evidence from the source. This is reinforced by using the phrase 'I know this because'.

Visual sources

You could also be asked to make inferences from a visual source – either a poster or cartoon or photograph. The approach will be the same – make an inference and support it with evidence.

Question 2: Causation

Below is an example of an exam-style causation question which is worth 12 marks.

Explain why the Montgomery Bus Boycott was a success.

> You may use the following in your answer:
> - The leadership of Martin Luther King
> - Media publicity
>
> You **must** also use information of your own.

How to answer

You need to explain at least three causes. This could be the two mentioned in the question and one of your own. You don't have to use the points given in the question, you could decide to make more points of your own instead. Try not to panic if you do not have any knowledge on the points given on the exam paper – simply don't use them. It is better to choose the points you know about which relate to the question rather than using the ones suggested.

Below is a sample answer to this question with comments around it.

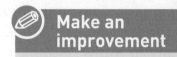

Make an improvement

Try improving the answer.

Martin Luther King was a very significant figure in organising the Bus Boycott of 1955. He was a very inspirational speaker and attacked the segregation of the South in America. His most famous speech was his 'I Have a Dream' speech made in Washington in 1963. With Martin Luther King's help, the Supreme Court declared Montgomery's bus laws to be illegal in 1956.

The Montgomery Bus Boycott was a high profile civil rights protest during which African Americans refused to ride city buses in Montgomery, Alabama. It was shown on television and radio throughout America and the rest of the world too. This encouraged many other Americans to turn against the idea of segregation in the American South and made it easier to encourage further change later on. It is also important that the media showed that non-violent direct action campaigning worked to challenge discrimination by refusing to cooperate with it.

- Martin Luther King is described. However, there is no explicit focus on the question.
- The supporting evidence is not precise enough.
- The answer is losing focus on the question.
- The Montgomery Bus is described. However, there is no explicit focus on the question – why was it a success?
- The supporting evidence is not precise enough.
- The answer is losing focus on the question.

A third cause is not explained.

Exam tip

Writing a good paragraph to explain an answer to something is as easy as **PEE**ing – Point, Example, Explain.

Your point is a short answer to the question. You then back this up with lots of examples to demonstrate all the knowledge you have learned during your studies: this is the section that proves you have studied and revised, rather than just

guessing. Finally, you will link that knowledge to the question by explaining in a final sentence:
- **P**oint: Passing my GCSE History exam will be very helpful in the future.
- **E**xample: For example, it will help me to continue my studies next year.
- **E**xplain: This will help me to get the job I want in the future.

Have a go

Now have a go at the following causation question:

Explain why there was progress in education for black Americans in the 1950s.

> You may use the following in your answer:
> - Little Rock High School
> - *Brown v Topeka*
>
> You **must** also use information of your own.

Question 3(a): Utility

Below is an example of an exam-style utility question. It is worth 8 marks.

How useful are Sources B and C for an enquiry into the US opposition to the conflict in Vietnam?

SOURCE B

A student slogan against the war in Vietnam.

Hey! Hey! LBJ [President Lyndon B Johnson]

How many kids did you kill today?

We don't want your war

Draft beer, not boys

Dump Johnson

Eighteen today, dead tomorrow

SOURCE C

General Westmoreland, who commanded the US forces in Vietnam until 1968, gave his views on the US media in 1979.

Actions by opponents of the war in the United States were supported by the news media. The media, no doubt, helped to back up the message that the war was 'illegal' and 'immoral'. Then came the enemy's Tet Offensive of early 1968. The North Vietnamese and Vietcong suffered a military defeat. Despite this, reporting of the offensive by the press and television in the USA gave the impression of an endless war that could never be won.

How to answer

- Explain the value and limitations of the contents of each source and try to add some contextual knowledge when you make a point.

- Explain the value and limitations of the NOP (Nature, Origin and Purpose) of each source and try to add some contextual knowledge when you make a point.

- In your conclusion, give a final judgement on the relative value of each source. For example, one source might provide one view of an event, the other source a different view.

✎ You're the examiner

1 Below are a mark scheme and a paragraph which is part of an answer to the question above at the top of this page. Read the paragraph and the mark scheme. Decide which level you would award the paragraph. Give a justification for your choice.

Mark scheme		
Level	Mark	
1	1–2	A simple judgement on utility is given, and supported by undeveloped comment on the content of the sources and/or their provenance
2	3–5	Judgements on source utility for the specified enquiry are given … related to the content of the sources and/or their provenance
3	6–8	Judgements on source utility for the specified enquiry are given … with developed reasoning which takes into account how the provenance affects the usefulness of the source content

Source B is useful because it suggests that many Americans protested against the actions of Lyndon Johnson, the US President at the time. This is shown by the lines: 'Hey! Hey! LBJ, How many kids did you kill today?' I know that Johnson refused to run for election in 1968 because of this pressure. However, it does have some limitations.

Source C is useful because it suggests a number of reasons why the Americans lost the Vietnam War, focusing mainly on the role of the media. From my own knowledge, I know that media figures like Walter Cronkite took a very negative view of the Vietnam War and gruesome images like those of the My Lai Massacre of 1968 were often displayed on American televisions. This had the effect of turning public opinion against the war. Source C is also useful because it is written by a general.

Level ☐ Reason _____

_____

2 Below is part of a high level answer to the question on page 43 which explains the utility of Source C. Read it and the comments around it.

Source C is useful because it suggests a number of reasons why the Americans lost the Vietnam War, focusing mainly on the role of the media. It says 'actions by opponents of the war in the United States were supported by the news media'. From my own knowledge, I know that media figures like Walter Cronkite took a very negative view of the Vietnam War and gruesome images like those of the My Lai Massacre of 1968 were often displayed on American televisions. This had the effect of turning public opinion against the war. However, the provenance of this source diminishes the utility of this source. It was written by General Westmoreland who, despite being in a position of knowledge regarding the Vietnam War, has a clear reason to despise the US media. He was often criticised in the US media for his strategies and therefore would perhaps over-emphasise the role the media played in the US defeat and shift the focus away from his own failing military strategies.

> A judgement is made on the value of the contents of the source.

> Own knowledge is used to support this judgement.

> The provenance of the source is taken into account when making a judgement on its utility.

3 On a separate piece of paper, write your own high level answer on Source B. Remember to take into account how the provenance affects the usefulness of the source content.

Question 3(b): How interpretations differ

REVISED ☐

Below is an example of an exam-style question 3(b) on the difference between two interpretations. It is worth 4 marks.

Study Interpretations 1 and 2. They give different views of US opposition to the conflict in Vietnam. What is the main difference between these views? Explain your answer, using details from both interpretations.

INTERPRETATION 1

From America Since 1945: The American Moment *by P. Levine and H. Papasotiriou, published in 2010.*

The anti-war movement's strongholds were the colleges, especially the elite universities, where student activities protested against the war with a visibility out of proportion to their numbers. Given that many anti-war students came from middle-class families supportive of the war, the result was a fierce generational confrontation.

INTERPRETATION 2

From Vietnam: A History *by S. Karnow, published in 1992.*

The spectacular Tet Offensive trapped President Johnson. His popularity had been dwindling for years, partly because of the war. When Tet came, his ratings plummeted – as if Vietnam was a burning fuse that had suddenly ignited an explosion of dissent. The country's trust in his authority had evaporated.

How to answer

You need to identify the main view that each interpretation has about US opposition to the conflict in Vietnam and explain each view. Below is an answer to this question which explains how the interpretations differ.

> A main difference is that Interpretation 1 emphasises the role students played in opposing the Vietnam War. It stresses that despite being a small group of the population, they were a very visible and loud protest group. On the other hand, Interpretation 2 emphasises the significance of the Tet Offensive in causing opposition to the Vietnam War, in particular how it impacted on Johnson's popularity. The main difference is therefore that Interpretation 1 focuses on the main group opposed to the war and Interpretation 2 gives reasons for that opposition.

> The main view of Interpretation 1 is identified and explained.

> The main view of Interpretation 2 is identified and explained.

Question 3(c): Why interpretations differ

REVISED

Below is an example of question 3(c) on the reasons why the two interpretations differ. It is worth 4 marks.

Suggest one reason why Interpretations 1 and 2 give different views about the US opposition to the conflict in Vietnam. You may use Sources B and C (see page 43) to help explain your answer.

How to answer

There are three reasons as to why the two interpretations differ. You only need to give one of these.

- The interpretations may differ because they have given weight to the two different sources. You need to identify the views given in the two sources and match these to the different interpretations.
- The interpretations may differ because they are partial extracts and in this case they do not actually contradict one another.
- They may differ because the authors have a different emphasis.

Below is part of an answer to this question in which the student uses the first option – they give different weight to different sources.

> The interpretations may differ because they give different weight to different sources. For example, Source B provides some support for Interpretation 2, which stresses the unpopularity of President Johnson by referring to the 'LBJ' chant.

> Interpretation 1 is matched to Source B.

> The view given in Source C is explained.

 Have a go

Now, on a separate piece of paper, complete this answer by matching Interpretation 2 to one of the sources.

Question 3(d): How far do you agree with one of the interpretations?

REVISED

Below is an example of an exam-style question 3(d) which asks you to make a judgement about how far you agree with one of the interpretations. It is worth 20 marks.

How far do you agree with Interpretation 2 about US opposition to the conflict in Vietnam? Explain your answer, using both interpretations and your knowledge of the historical context.

How to answer

You need to give a balanced answer which agrees and disagrees with the interpretation using evidence from the two interpretations as well as your own knowledge. Here is one way you could approach this:

- agree with the view with evidence from Interpretation 2
- agree with the view with evidence from your own knowledge
- disagree with the view with evidence from Interpretation 1
- disagree with the view with evidence from your own knowledge
- make a final judgment on the view.

Below is part of an answer to this question in which the student agrees with the view given in Interpretation 2.

I agree with the view given in Interpretation 2 about the reasons for US opposition to the Vietnam War. The interpretation suggests that military factors such as the Tet Offensive caused opposition against the war which shows itself in Johnson's plummeting popularity rating. I know from my own knowledge that Johnson refused to stand for election in 1968 because of his unpopularity.

> The answer immediately focuses on the question.

> Support is provided from Interpretation 2 for this view.

> Own knowledge is used to provide support for the view.

I agree with the statement that the Tet Offensive 'trapped' Johnson. For the first few years of the war, Johnson had been convincing the US people that the war in Vietnam was being won. However, on 30 January 1968, thousands of Vietcong troops attacked US positions in South Vietnam, managing to capture the US embassy in Saigon and attacking over 100 town and cities, with fierce fighting around the city of Hué. Despite the US forces eventually forcing the attack back, the media had already circulated horrific images of the US embassy siege and South Vietnamese officers shooting Vietcong prisoners. This, with the impact of the My Lai Massacre soon after, had the impact of decisively turning public opinion against the war and against Johnson. Therefore I agree with Interpretation 2 because it is clear that the events of 1968 proved that Johnson was misleading the American people about the success of the Vietnam War and his reputation was shattered because of this.

 Have a go

Now, on a separate piece of paper, have a go at writing the rest of the answer by disagreeing with the view given in Interpretation 2. Remember to write a conclusion giving your final judgement on the question. Here is an example of a good conclusion.

Overall, I mostly agree with Interpretation 2 about reasons for US opposition to the war. It is clear from the beginning that the Vietnam War was unwinnable from a military standpoint, as highlighted by the Tet Offensive, referred to in Interpretation 2. However, without a significant group of potential protesters available at home, as highlighted by Interpretation 1's references to the students, there would never have been such an explosion of popular unrest in reaction to this military disaster.